The Weber Family

Of

Beal City, Michigan

THE WEBER FAMILY OF BEAL CITY MICHIGAN

ORSB Publishing

POB 16 Mount Pleasant, Michigan, 48804-0016

989-773-5741

Copyright 2014 by Jack R. Westbrook

ISBN: 10- 09484036156

ISBN 13/EAN 13 978-0-09840361-5-8

ON THE COVER

Author Ben Weber welcomes guests at the Weber Beal City Museum during the Isabella County 150th Anniversary celebration in 2009. In 2014, The museum is still open to the public upon request at Weber Brother Sawmill (ask at the mill for free admission).

DEDICATION

Dedicated to Jeffrey John Weber, who succumbed Tuesday, June 4, 2013 at 57 years old. Jeff shared his father's passion for history.

The Weber Family

Of

Beal City, Michigan

By Ben J. Weber

Edit & Design by Jack R. Westbrook

ORSB PUBLISHING
Mt. Pleasant MI

THE WEBER FAMILY OF BEAL CITY MICHIGAN

Beal City, seen above from the air in 1947, was a nameless settlement around a lumber camp starting in 1875. Beal City was unnamed for many years. In 1881, Nicholas Beal built the first general store and hosted the first Beal City post office in the southeast corner of section 21, Nottawa Township, Isabella County, Michigan.

In his 1911 *"Past and Present of Isabella County, Michigan"*, Mt. Pleasant Isaac A. Fancher said of the community:

"Beal City is another small hamlet of a few houses, store and post office, a Catholic Church and parochial school. It is in the center of one of the very best of farming communities. It is settled largely with Germans, a thrifty, prosperous and intelligent class. This is one of the places in the county that you can stand on a raise of ground and count from one spot nine large round- roofed farm barns, a sight that is seldom witnessed anywhere in the state, or in any other state. It speaks volumes for their industry and thrift."

THE WEBER FAMILY OF BEAL CITY MICHIGAN

Founded in 1882, just six years before Moritz Weber bought property in Nottawa County. Saint Philomena Catholic Parish had two fires destroy their church before the present structure was completed and consecrated in 1907. In 1961, the name of the parish was changed to St. Joseph the Worker. The Weber family has long, strong ties to the parish. Below, young Ben Weber *(third from the right below)* was part of the 1950s St. Philomena choir when it competed in Big Rapids.

Right to left is: Dick Smith, organist Geraldine Horn, Ben Weber, Lavern Schafer, Marvin Pasch, Art Faber, Ray Gross and Chum Schafer

Along with helping make the history of Beal City, the Webers have displayed pride in that history, exhibiting historic memorabilia in their barn-museum and on the lawn of the Weber Centennial Farm, *below*.

INTRODUCTION

This is not meant to be a great literary work. It is written merely to trace the path of the Weber family from as far back as I could go. This is the first 6 chapters, which took me about five years to do. To wait till it is all done might be another fifteen years, so I thought it best to distribute this much at this time

— Ben J. Weber – date Unknown.

EDITORS NOTE

The above was written by Ben J. Weber at an unknown period of modern times. At this publication, Ben lives, but health issues preclude his finishing this quest to bring the Weber family narrative to fruition.

About four years ago, Ben knocked on my back door. I've known Ben since we were fellow members of Mt. Pleasant, Michigan's first Toastmasters Club in the mid-1960s and we've since maintained a "Hi, how are you" casual relationship. 2009, I visited his Beal City Museum in the barn at the family sawmill. I had published my "Isabella County 1859-1879" book the previous year and Ben knew of my interest in all things local history, so he brought me the raw manuscript. "Don't know who'd be interested but I thought you'd like to see this." Ben said in typical wry modest fashion while I scanned the Jacob Weber 1 oil well pictures in this volume. I was interested Ben, enough to want to help you share the Weber story herein with the world.

The narrative is presented exactly as Ben wrote it.

Jack R. Westbrook, March 18, 2014

Table of Contents

INTRODUCTION 6
EDITORS NOTE 6
REVELATION 8
IN TRANSITION 18
AND IN THE BEGINNING 31
LEARNING OF THE "AMERICAN WAY." 51
ESTABLISHING A HOMESTEAD 67
THE BLESSING OF THE WEBER 1 WELL 87
CALIFORNIA GOLD 89
About the Author 110

Chapter 1

REVELATION

It was a dark and stormy night. The German friend I had just met that night said "Ah, you are Swabian." When our friends Ralph and Elaine O'Neil asked Shirley and me if we would accompany them on a trip to Germany in August of 1978, we eagerly accepted. Well, maybe Shirley wasn't as eager as I was but it was a dream of mine to go to Germany.

Here was an excellent opportunity. Elaine and Ron had volunteered to house two German students in their home prior to that. One, Gerod Gomer was a teacher in Germany and was taking some summer classes at Central Michigan University in Mt. Pleasant. He was about 27, married, and a friendly person who knew his way around. The other was a high school student named Fritz. He came over as an exchange student and attended Beal City High School, the eleventh and twelfth grades. They had both expressed a desire for Elaine and Ron to visit them in Germany, as they had become fast friends. It was an excellent opportunity for us and especially to have two guides and interpreters while there.

On landing at Frankfort, Fritz picked us up in his father's German car, an Opal or something, anyway, it wasn't all that big and we had a passel of luggage. Each time we packed, we had an awful time getting everything packed in. We traveled to Gerod's home at Erding, which was about 8 miles north of Munich. We spent three or four days in an inn there. The rooms were above the combination bar and restaurant, and they had a courtyard where you could drink or have parties. It was a swell place and we enjoyed our time there. The waitresses were real friendly and made us feel at home. We drank much beer there. We went out from there to visit Munich and other points of interest in the area. Fritz had gone into Munich to visit a friend and Gerod took over as our guide. He had no car so we traveled by train. Gerod had an apartment about three blocks from our hotel, and the last night we were there he had a barbecue party in the back yard of his apartment. This was the dark and starless night and the only light was a candle in the center of the picnic table. He had invited a few friends, one of them was a connoisseur of fine wines who traveled to an area of Northern Italy which at one time was a part of the German Empire and had German settlers that had remained there. That's where he went to pick up his supply of wine. It was real good.

In our old Family Possessions, I had found a bunch of old postcards addressed to my Grandfather Moritz Weber from relatives in Germany that had postmarks of 1919 and 1920. I had slipped them into my shirt pocket on leaving home. At different times I had tried to get people to read them, but I was told they were written in the old dialect and they didn't understand it. I took them out at this party and asked Gerod if anyone there could read them. I explained the connection of the cards to my kin and all. One of his friends was a lawyer who easily read the cards, and after reading a couple of them, said, "Ah, you are Swabian." Germany at the time of Christ was made up of many tribes, Kingdoms, Duchies, etc., but about the 6th Century A.D. only six main tribes remained there. East Franks were in the valleys of the lower Rhine and Meuse Rivers. The Saxons in north Germany with the small Thuringian tribe wedged in between them and the Franks! The ancient Suevi, now called Swabia was spread over the angle made by the upper waters of the Danube and the Rhine and were settled even upon the flanks of the Alps and Jural Mountains! The Bavarians lay along the middle Danube between the Lech and Inn rivers.

This home of the Swabian was in the southwest part of Germany, and this was the area that these cards were sent from. To the people living in Germany these old tribal divisions of Germany were very much alive and important, although in name- dead long ago, as the rest of the world never hears of them. I suppose it is like the Cajuns of Louisiana, or the Amish, Indians, or the red necks in Georgia and so on. All good Americans to the rest of the world- but we know the quirks and ways and idiosyncrasies of all these different peoples. To us they are all from their distinct area and if someone says Amish we instantly paint a picture of them and can say any number of things about them to make them stand out as a so called separate tribe in this country.

Well, that's the way the Swabians are to a German. Gerod and his friends them proceeded to tell about the ways of my kinfolk the Swabians. They are very strongly Catholic and don't live far from the church. They are clannish and tend to settle in one area or place and don't generally move around. They tend to like the plot that they own and generally think it is better than their neighbors or other land in the area. They tend to be in an occupation associated with agriculture, like farming or forestry. As they were painting the picture, I could easily see my reflection and I said, "Yes, we Weber's are Swabian." How all these traditions and ways of people can transcend oceans and time and all, and here we are living by and carrying on these traditions and ways, unbeknownst during all these years that we are descended to it. It is interesting to note that the history of feudal Germany begins with the complete union of the Five Great Germany Tribes- Franks, Swabians, Bavarians, Thuringians and Saxons under the Carolingian Dynasty in the 6th Century. But this was a tribal union, never a tribal consolidation. No ruling house in Germany has ever succeeded in overcoming this original and primordial heterogeneity of the German race. A common blood a common speech, and a common body of institutions have never canceled this sense of separate tribal identity among the German peoples.

After noting the village where this postcard was mailed from, Gerod's lawyer friend asked Fritz, who had rejoined us as we were leaving the next day, which way we were traveling from there. Fritz told him we were going south to Oberammergau and the Zugspitz, and then west and north through Ulm, ending up at Fritz's folk's home at Braunlage. He said, "Why don't you go up through this village and maybe you can find some of the relatives there?" Fritz said yes we can and we had time and so we did. We crammed everything in Fritz's car and then headed south. Elaine had done a lot of research on Germany and had an itinerary all worked out. We took the cable car up the Zugspitz, which is the highest peak in the Bavarian Alps and the highest in Germany. I brought a small rock back from there; it's in the fireplace at the Evart cabin. Then on to Obrammergau- the site of the Passion Play and much woodcarving. We went through an old castle and saw many things that were new and interesting to us. The roads were good, we had been taking a lot of secondary roads to see more of the real Germany. Now we were on the Autobahn and Heidenheim going north through Ulm. Just south of Aalen and a little west are the villages of Unterkochen, Ebnat, and Walhausen, the villages where my kinfolk come from and where the postcards had been sent from in 1919 and 1929. We didn't know where to start looking. We went to a Catholic Church about a mile out of Unterkochen and inquired at the rectory but the priest was not there and the housekeeper was not very friendly and gave us no help. We went looking around and saw a cemetery a little way from the church. It was on a gentle hill overlooking the surrounding countryside. We were there perhaps an hour looking at the names on the tombstones. There were quite a few Webers there and I was copying down dates of births and deaths. We were scattered out through the cemetery and I was near the center along a footpath that went from the church to the far end of the cemetery and out into the countryside. I looked up as an older woman and child walked toward me heading in the direction of the church.

They stopped and she said something to me in German. She was waiting for me to reply but of course I couldn't understand.

I motioned for Fritz to come over and see what she wanted. She had said, "Whom do you seek?" Fritz told her and she said she knew the Webers and she pointed toward the village of Unterkochen, which was about a mile away. But we couldn't see it as it was in a small valley surrounded by rolling hills. One of my postcards had a picture of this village and someone had inked an "x" on the roof of one of the ten houses in the village. We drove to the house but we were one house off because they had built one house there since the picture had been taken 60 years before. We went next door then and two older ladies were there and they were my kinfolk. Word of our arrival had spread through the village like wildfire and the villagers all gathered around. All the houses were right up to the street and that's where the gathering was. I never heard so much jabbering and carrying on and hugging. After a while the people went back to their homes and we went inside their house. They fetched out two bottles of fine wine and we sat around the table visiting and drinking. One of the postcards I had showed two girls aged 3 and 5, and two boys 6and 8 years old. One lady looked at it and said it was her and her sister. Then she went to her cupboard and found a picture postcard exactly like the one I had in my hand. She had duplicates of some of the rest of the cards too. Fritz was sure busy translating.

These two ladies were Granddaughters of my Grandfather Moritz Weber's sister Walburga Siegel.

Their names were Theresa Zoller and Marie (last name unknown). Theresa's son Anton Zoller stopped by and we visited with him also. His wife's name is Bridgett and they had two children, Tom and Sarah, who was born the day before we were there. This meeting took place in early afternoon and they advised us to get accommodations for the night at Ebnat. Our rooms were above a bar and that was just dandy, a real nice place. Shirley and Elaine chose to stay there, while Fritz, Ron and I went the four miles to Waldhausen to see the old Weber Homestead. Anton had told us it was near a church. We went to the Catholic Church and only the housekeeper was home. She was an older lady and very helpful.

As we stood on the porch talking to her, the neighbor lady across the street came out on her porch and hollered across, "What's going on?" The housekeeper hollered back. "They are from America looking for the old Weber Farm."

Now this neighbor was quite old, I thought about 70 or so, and she said, "I don't know, but I'll ask my mother," and she went inside. She was back in a few minutes and said that it was right next door to her house where a bank now stood. A nice looking bank was there and right across the street from the church. I walked around the place and trod on the soil that I knew my ancestors had trod and toiled on. It was quite an emotional experience. I tried to visualize how bad conditions were here and the hardships the people had to endure to try to earn a living and practice their religion. It didn't seem to me that they were asking for all that much. It seemed like such a peaceful place and everything was kept up neat and all.

The housekeeper invited us in and said she would see if she could find the records of the family since she was not only the housekeeper, but the bookkeeper as well. She went upstairs and found the names, back to about 1780 with the birth of Franz Anton Weber and Maria Anna Weber, born Dambacher. There was no record of birth or death on them, since this was before such records were kept. This was my Grandfather Moritz Weber's Grandparents. She followed it through four generations to Jacob Weber who dies in 1950 and this Jacob in Germany was the same generation as my father Jacob Weber who died in 1967.

I left my address with her because she said she would go to Aalen the county seat, and get an official record of my ancestors. She did and she sent it to me…Many thanks to her. We left there very ecstatic with the information we were getting. I just couldn't believe all this was actually taking place. Fritz was such a great help and really took a personal interest in it.

We drove back to Ebnat and had a couple beers and supper. Then all the relative living in the area came to the bar and we had a party. Didn't we have a party? It was a shot of schnapps and beer all evening. They close the bars in Germany at about 10 o'clock, which was a good thing. The next morning we had a picture taking session and some more relatives were there that couldn't make it the night before. It was uncanny the resemblance of these people to us Weber's here. Especially Theresa and Maria, the first two we met. They so resembled my Aunts Katie and Mary, in their speech mannerisms, smiles, and the way they folded their arms. And this one guy Jacob Weber, (they had a Jacob in about every generation), so looked like my Dad, Jacob. It meant a lot to me for Shirley, Ron, Elaine, and Fritz to take a day from a busy schedule for this search of my ancestors. I'm very thankful.

It was time to move on.

We said our good-byes and went to Fritz's parent's home at Braunlage, which is right near the Iron Curtain. We stayed there for two nights, and they showed us the sights of the area. We went then to Koblenz and took a boat tour on the Rhine River north to Mainz. It was very picturesque with the vineyards and old castles. This boat ride was a leisurely ending to our stay in Germany.

The best part of the trip was following up on the words of Gerod's friend; "You are Swabian." I am very thankful for the seemingly simple things the Lord has done for me to open doors and passageways for me to pass through on this quest of tracing my ancestor's paths.

That woman and little girl in the cemetery had no business being there. It looked like no one had passed that way in days and they seemed to appear from nowhere.

They had no business stopping to ask a foreign stranger, "Who do you seek?"

Yes, they can spot a foreigner from a distance.

And how did she know what she did? Gomer's friend after all the people I showed those postcards to could read them.

Why did I ask him?

He had to read by candlelight. My Dad always said, "The Lord works in mysterious ways, his wonders to perform."

Chapter II
IN TRANSITION

In this age of historical, ethnological, anthropological and philological research, to write a complete history of the Swabian Tribe of Germany, of which the Weber's are descendants, would require the lifetime of a man trained in these particular branches of study. That duty must be left to men of more leisure, and with a greater capacity and love for delving in to tomes of musty lore than this author claims to possess.

Therefore, I only hope to give a short sketch of the Swabians from the earliest days of their known existence, to the time of the migrations to America and then their influence on life in this country up to the present time. In order to better understand why we are as we are today, I feel it necessary to give the reader a general idea of the origin, geographical situation in Europe, the early conditions, the customs and laws of this ancient people. I am including this information for one purpose to better understand why so many good citizens could leave their native land as my Grandparents did, and go to a strange land and start over with only the shirt on their backs and visions of better things.

A quote from "The Races of Man" by J. Deniker-

THE WEBER FAMILY OF BEAL CITY MICHIGAN

"Of all parts of the world, Europe presents the most favorable conditions for the interblending of Peoples. Easy of access, a mere peninsula of Asia from which the Ural mountains and straits a few miles wide hardly separate it, Europe has a totally different configurations from the continental colossus, heavy and vague in outline, to which it is attached. Indented by numerous gulfs, bays and creeks, provided with several secondary peninsulas, crossed by rivers having no cataracts, and for the most part navigable, it offers every facility for communication and change of place to ethnic groups. Thus from the dawn of history, and even from prehistoric times, a perpetual eddying has taken place there, a coming and going of peoples in search of fortune and better settlements. These migrations, combined with innumerable wars and active commerce, have provided such a blending of races, such successive changes in the manners and customs and languages spoken, that it is very difficult to separate from this chaos the elements of European Ethnogeny.

"And Germany was the center of it all, the crossroads of Europe. The Kelts, Angles, Saxons, Jutes, Goths, Vandals, Burgundians, and many others migrated across Germany, some settling, some moving on, all of them leaving their mark by taking wives and husbands with those already living there. And all the while battles and wars were fought starting with the tribes, duchies, and fiefdoms, the victors taking captive women and children. Later on countries fought over and across Germany many times and Germany was usually in the middle of the fray. It took a long time for German land to become German

land and nothing else; this started about the year 800. Cooperation of the temporal rulers with the clergy of the Roman church was in large part responsible for reorganizing the tribes into forming Germany.

Germany was an area that was very productive in natural resources. It was a very good farming area and their forests were legend. The Black Forest was in the area of the Swabian Tribe. There was much wild game in the area and the people hunted for food and furs.

Germans were main tillers of the soil and it being a good climate they could maintain a good livelihood without seasonal migrations. This then became the first area of Europe to have a more cereal and vegetable diet and having homes where cooking could done, while other nationalities were still pulling raw meat from bones with their teeth. People living in an early cultural state use the teeth as tools for gnawing, tearing, and manipulating substances other than food. This secondary use of the teeth was gradually abandoned with the adoption of hand held implements. The importance of the incisors as reducing and tearing tools were gradually reduced as the molars became increasingly used for the grinding and chewing of grain.

An anthropological study of human skulls of the early inhabitants of Germany reveal that their jaws come together with what is called an overbite, which is when the top front teeth come down in front of the lower teeth. This indicates that for hundreds of years, they cooked meat or ate cereal and vegetable, ground up by the back molars.

Whereas anywhere else, the front teeth naturally came together even, more for tearing flesh. It is interesting to note that while, for instance, Orientals have basically the same skull size and bone structure as do all the other basic cultures, Germany is apt to have a lot of differences. They have both tall and short individuals, round headed and narrow headed, broad faced and long faced, snub nosed and sharp nosed, fair headed and dark haired, brown eyed and blue eyed, they are found in every corner of the nation. People with blue eyes came from ancestors who lived where the sun shone not so steadily. People with brown eyes came from ancestors who lived where the sun shone most of the time. This is true, theoretically, the scholars say, but humans have been so mongrelized it doesn't really mean much." No other great European people are woven of so many different strands as the Germans. And author John Gerpel wrote, "Man arrived in Europe a mongrel and mongrels we remain."

Germany was a good climate and landscape for permanent settlement and the German has been distinguished by his very deep love of his native spot. The German soul clung to the maternal warmth of just this little bit of Earth. A great point is the feeling of rootedness of connection. I want to explain this rootedness of connection business. To me it is very important. These are the things instilled in us, either material or words (linguistic) ideas that we observed or gotten from our parents or ancestors, that we pass on to our children and they to their children's children. This is the connection from one generation to another, which makes the roots of a family tree. This makes a strong family and one that the members have a strong feeling for. It also is their rootedness to their particular little plot of this Earth.

Serfdom remained an institution in Germany until 1500 or 1600 A.D., and was still strong up to 1850. Servility is deep in the German's blood. The lower classes have always been systematically exploited, tyrannized over, were ill-treated and humiliated.

If you were born a commoner you had no chance to better yourself. The mass of Germans were most successfully constrained by the Class-Caste system. If you were born a nobleman, you could do anything and a commoner had to bow to him and step off the path and let him pass by. The people did not do, too bad in old Feudal Germany in their old free towns. But later they were preyed upon by petty dukes and princes. These leaches preyed on the citizens by demanding payment for safe passages and protection. This pretty much kept them in servitude. It kept the people poor paying tribute to the princes and dukes and kings.

I never did realize the tremendous influence of the Catholic Church in Europe in general and Germany in particular. For hundreds of years it was known as The Holy Roman Empire at its zenith covered about all of Europe and parts of Asia and Africa. For many years in Germany the bishops and clergy about ruled Germany, and gained control over vast areas of land and holdings. The people were obligated to support this vast Empire, else they would have had a hard time getting to paradise.

Martin Luther forever changed the churches picture in Germany and the world. This started the "reformation." I went 12 years in a Catholic School and I'll never forget that every time the "reformation" was mentioned it was always called, "the So-Called Reformation." As if to say there wasn't anything to reform. Well, after reading about the history of Germany and conditions there. I'd say that there was no cause to call it "the So-Called Reformation." There certainly was reforming to do. And the Church settled in more to do what it was intended to do, administer to the spiritual side of man. The German Americans are among the soundest citizen of their great adoptive country and they have attained extraordinary successes in all provinces of its life. The reason may have been that these immigrants came under the tutelage of a strong constitution and a healthy democratic spirit, privileges which they had missed in the fatherland and which their former fellow countrymen and been unable adequately to create.

Here I want to tell some of the things particular to German people of which Swabia is a part.

Why are Germans called Germans?

When their ancient forefathers entered battle, they shouted, yelled, and hollered a lot, and the Gauls called them "Germans," from a Celtic word meaning "to shout." German people were known by other nationalities as men of iron in battle. They also compared the shouting of Germans in battle to the roaring of lions. An Italian traveling in Germany in Saxon times wrote of German music at this time: "These men on the other side of the Alps, when they let the hunger of their voices rise rumbling to the sky, never are they able to attain any sweetness of modulation, the roughness of their wine guzzling throats is barbaric and whenever they try, by lowering and then raising their voices, to express a melodious softness, nature shudders for it sounds like the creaking of cart wheels over frozen earth."

Louis Kornexl was our neighbor and my Godfather who lived on the Paul Schafer place when I was a boy, he talked German about all of the time. The words came out of his mouth like scraggly hunks of iron. My Uncle Ernest Schmidt told this tale. Clement Starr who lived just east of Beal, was cutting brush with an axe on the edge of a swamp. It was real cold and the axe probably wasn't too sharp. A branch of brush swatted his face, stinging terribly, he raised his axe to the swamp and hollered in German, "You whole swamp I will do battle."

The Swabians were noted as the toughest, stockiest, and most hardworking of the German Tribes. One episode in particular shows this. At the siege of Weinsberg in Swabia a well-known and well substantiated episode took place. King Conrad III allowed the women to depart unmolested on condition that they themselves should carry off their own most precious possessions, whereupon they carried away their husbands. The king was amazed, but he didn't retract his word in the face of this bold interpretation and the men were spared.

Many Germans make use of wakes for the dead, and christenings for the newborn as the Irish do. However a man dies, so the saying goes, be he suicide, accident, victim, or the prey of old age, he will be washed to the shores of the Great Beyond on the waves of alcohol.

Count Von Flemming said, *"The farther east you go, the larger the schnapps glasses get, and the smaller the washbasins."*

Albert Einstein was a Swabian, whose kin inhabited the foothills of the Swabian Alps for 150 years. He was inevitably drawn to America because it offered safety from Totalitarian Police, solitude, and a free forum for his thoughts and something more…*"A country where political liberty, toleration and equality of all citizens before the law is the rule."* He said of his family, *"If there were talents or gifts among them, they could not, because of the restricted conditions of life, express them."* Einstein held off becoming a citizen of America several years.

As Historian Dr. Paul Forman wrote, *"The U.S. is a jealous nation, it demands that aliens renounce all other political allegiances before admission to its citizenship, and Einstein didn't cotton to that."*

Mr. Einstein gives many reasons in regards to why I am covering some of the past history of Germany, which is to try to better understand why so many citizens left their native land for America.

Napoleon crossed Germany in his conquests getting recruits from the native peoples. I remember some of the old family stories connected with this. Napoleon recruited many of his personal Army troops from the German Tribes. As he was short of stature, he sought out the tallest of men for his honor guard. My one early kin was well over six feet tall and was picked for this duty. One requirement was to grow a full beard, and one trait of my family is some of the males just can't grow a good full beard, the facial hair just sprouts here and there. My father Jacob Weber was thus, also my sister Kathryn's son Chris has this trait. Well, my kin had the same problem and Napoleon didn't like that and as Germans in general were noted for their hairy bodies, he couldn't figure why my kin didn't. So, he posted a guard on him 24 hours a day to see if he shaved on the sly. He didn't of course and was kept on. It was considered a great honor to serve in this honor guard.

Another of my kin served with Napoleon across Europe to Russia where the harsh Russian winter got the best of them and they turned back defeated. In one fierce battle, it wasn't going too good and so my kin removed the entrails from a fallen horse and crawled inside the cavity while the battle raged about him. When things settled down, he crawled out and joined the victors. He lived by one of my father's favorite family sayings, "Expedience is the better part of valor."

I want to give a picture of the Rhine country and southwestern Germany during the period directly preceding the time of the greatest immigration from Germany to America. The most destructive of all wars that devastated Germany was the 30 Years War, none more terrible is known to history. It is an accepted fact that in its material development, Germany was set back two hundred years. Throughout Germany seventy five percent of the inhabitants were killed and the property loss was far greater. It was said, the army only left behind "Flowing iron and millstones."

This area was known as the Palatinate, and it was a passageway from France to Eastern Europe. France was a power at this time and the Palatinate was to be made and kept a desert in order not to serve as a granary for the enemies of France. A remarkable fact in the history of this area is that during the brief intervals of peace, between successive invasions the country showed most wonderful recuperative power. Whenever a period of ten years of peace was vouched safe, the country prospered to such an enormous degree, that it again became the alluring bait for warlike neighbors. The fertility of the soil, the industry, and the agriculture kill of the population, a nation of farmers through thirty generations, invariably transformed again the desert into a garden. The invading armies frequently took advantage of this ability to recover allowing just enough time to grow new crops again before reinvasion. On one occasion a French Army, after having robbed a district of everything it possessed, returned seeds to the farmers, so they might prepare another harvest for the soldiers. The farmers by and by refused to turn the sod and raise crops for others to reap.

Some of the rulers were tolerant in matters of religion, but most were not. If they were Catholic, they persecuted the Protestants, if they were Protestants, they persecuted the Catholics. They would confiscate church property, and the worshipers were expelled from the particular area.

Another main cause of the immigration was the tyranny of the princes of small domains. They thumb crewed their faithful subjects until they were reduced to serfdom or beggary. Not only did the princes tyrannously disregard the economic welfare of their subjects, but several of them added religious persecution to the other inflictions. All the more did the persecuted hold fast to their religion, whatever sect they belonged to Lutheran, Huguenots, Waldences, Mennonites, Quakers, Catholics, being all that was left then, a treasure that could not be attacked by dust or rust, or the lust of Princes.

A fond hope for betterment of their earthly condition then, rose in their hearts with good reports from the American Colonists. The wretchedness of their present condition, the impossibility of future improvement seeming never more evident as now, turned sentiment into resolution, and what might be likened to a tidal wave of immigration, from the banks of the Rhine to the shores of America, the Promised Land.

The perils of the immigrant by land and sea may serve to increase our admiration of the courage and heroism of the early immigrants and remind us also that neither cleverness nor gullibility was born in our own generation.

You can imagine the ignorance of the potential immigrant and the person they turned to was called a "Newlander." These individuals had been to America and then came back to Germany as immigrant agents either employed by ship Companies or in many cases acted on their own initiative. They not only obtained commissions from their employers, but had many opportunities of extracting money from the immigrants, who they pretended to serve as friends or patrons. These Newlanders prowled Germany to recruit all the people they could, enticing them with descriptive pamphlets and letters of testimony from people already settled in America. These pamphlets would paint a glowing picture of the glorious opportunities waiting in the New World. One in particular states that the land literally flows with milk and honey the cows roam about on perfect pasture all year round, and honey being found abundantly in hollow trees. Wild turkeys are found in flocks of five hundred, geese that some of the farmers possess in flocks to the number of 200, furnish choice feather beds. As for game, that bison put their heads though the windows of log cabins waiting to be shot.

Once these Newlanders got recruits then they would speedily arrange a plan of exit by way of the Rhine and the Netherlands. If an immigrant was without money, a plan was established to get him to the Promised Land. He would agree to serve from three to seven years in America until the price of this passage was paid off to the shipmaster that had advanced it. Buyers would bargain with the immigrants for a certain number of years and days depending upon the price demanded by the ship captain or merchant. As time went on, profits in transportation of these "redemptioners" as they were called were greater than the passengers who paid their way. Ways then were found to relieve the immigrants of their money before they got on ship.

They found the best places for this was on the passage down the Rhine. The number of toll stations was legion and a fee paid at each one. Fees were demanded with such frequency by agents of all kinds that the unhappy immigrant had little left by the time he got to board ship.

Such a struggle they had!

Chapter III
AND IN THE BEGINNING

The first official record of the Webers in Germany was of Franz Anton Weber and Marie Anna Weber born Dambacher. They were my Great-Great Grandparents. There is no way of knowing when they were born or when they died as civil registration of births, marriages, and deaths started in Germany in 1789, so any events before that time we have to go by later events and work backwards. Some churches kept records prior to that but not all were recorded.

The early record list Franz and Marie as being from the village of Beuron, Kingdom of Wuertenberg, Germany. They must have moved to the nearby village of Waldhausen and established a homestead as that's where their children were born and relatives still live there and in other nearby villages. Franz and Marie as far as I know had four sons and two daughters. We are going to be writing about two of them as they represent the two branches of the Webers history that we know about. They are Josef Weber, born 20 March 1804 and died 31 January 1872 and Michael Weber, born 12 September 1824, date of death is unknown. Now, going backwards, their father and mother, Franz and Marie were probably born about 1780 or 1785 as Josef was born in 1804 and Michael in 1824. Josef Weber married Katherina Weber born Sunder on the 3rd of August 1831. Katherina was born 21 April

1812 and died 29 October 1878. Her parents were Anton Sunder of Hulen and Victoria Sunder, born Brolle, of Waldhausen. Josef and Katherina were my Great Grandparents.

A social rule of Germany was that in the later years of a couple's life, they transfer everything over to the eldest son and in return, had to keep the old folks until they died. In this case it fell on Josef and Katherina to do this. The other siblings then could find their own way.

Following a decade of severe economic depression and famine, they had a full-scale revolution in Germany in 1848-1849. Due to dissension and quarreling among the revolutionary leaders, the rebellion was crushed and up to 19,000 Germans immigrated to America at this time. Among this group was Michael Weber, son of Franz Anton Weber and brother of my Great Grandfather Josef Weber. Michael arrived here on 12 June 1854 on the ship "Luna" from Bremen, Germany. He was 30 years old. Another passenger on the "Luna" was a girl named Ottilia Adelia Brenner from Dorf-Merkinger, Germany. She was born 26 December 1826.

The "Luna" was a sailing ship and all the passengers were required to bring along all the food they would need on the voyage and they were advised to be frugal with their food and not throw away any scraps. They found the reason why when they were becalmed for nearly a month and needed all the food scraps they had saved to eat. We don't know whether Michael and Ottilia knew each other before they sailed or if they met and fell in love on the

"Luna." A Father Jacger married them 4 July 1855 in Buffalo, New York.

They wended their way westward and settled on the northern tip of the Keweenaw Peninsula at Eagle Harbor, Michigan. The North American Copper mine was located near there and that's where Michael worked. He lost an eye at the mine and that was enough mining for him. He was a true Swabian and wanted his own little spot in the world where he could farm, raise a family and be able to practice his religion in peace. He found his place in Noble Township near Defiance, Ohio where he bought 80 acres for $1,000.00 that he had saved working in the copper mine. This was in 1861. He prospered and many of his kin live in that area.

The copper boom in the Keweenaw lasted for more than a century, from the 1840's to the 1960's. It was America's first great mining boom, predating even the California Gold Rush At one time the peninsula produced 80% of the world's copper supply. But along the way, it absorbed many setbacks; strikes, the Great Depression, corporate takeovers, and cheap competition that ultimately reduced it to a shadow of its former self and turned many thriving villages into ghost towns. Old timers who live there say the area will thrive again, as there is enough copper in the Keweenaw to supply the world for hundreds of years.

Michael and Ottilia Weber had three children born at Eagle Harbor and four born in Ohio. Their oldest son John and his wife Mary had eight children, two of which were George and Benedict, who was known as Nick. George and Nick moved to Midland, Michigan when they were of working age.

George' wife's name was Mayme, they lived two block from St. Bridget's Catholic Church in Midland. They had five daughters, three are living now in 1998, and they are Louise Schick, Irene Wazney, and Sister Margaret Weber who is a nun. Nick never married and lived in a shack east and north of Oil City on the corner of Castor and Huckleberry Rd. When Nick died he willed his property to the "Society for the Propagation of the Faith." This property was on the west side of Castor Rd. The Society must have sold it as it is listed under an individual name now. George had 80 acres across Castor Rd. to the east and is owned by his descendants, the Wazney's and Shicks who use it for deer hunting at this time. George worked at Dow Chemical Company for many years and retired from there.

I had tried for several years to figure out how we were related to the Webers in Midland, as my folks Jacob and Eleanor used to visit back and forth with them maybe two or three times a year. This summer, Louise Schick contacted me and with her information and my information we put it together. We met here with Louise, Irene, and Sr. Margaret. It was wonderful. Louise has been doing genealogy on their branch of the family since the 1960's. The reason I gave a rundown on this branch of the Weber family is because it is interesting and mainly it was important for Michael to be permanently settled in Ohio when my Grandfather Moritz and his brother Johan

George Weber immigrated to America in 1872. The redemptionist business had ended earlier and was replaced by the sponsorship. Michael had wrote to his brother in Germany and said he would be a sponsor for the boys if they came to America. Ship passage cost about $100.00 at this time and you had to have at least $25.00 cash in hand on landing so you wouldn't be stranded in New York, which was really a problem for emigration authorities. This $25.00 was enough to get you to your sponsor and then you were his responsibility.

When Michael immigrated to America he could see no future in the political upheavals and warfare in Germany. He was not as bound by social traditions and rules as his brother Josef, my Great Grandfather. Josef and Katherina's future was sealed in Germany. They had a 15 acre farm in the village of Waldhausen. On these 15 acres, they had a home barn combination, which is common in Germany to this day, 15 cattle, 4 cows, 2 horses, 10 pigs, 20 chickens and a flock of geese. This had to support Grandparents if living, parents and children. In true Swabian style this farm was across the road from the Catholic Church. Josef and Katherina had five children, Jacob the eldest, then Walburga, Josef Jr., Johan (George), and the youngest my Grandfather Moritz. The father Josef was quite intelligent and passed it on to his children. This family did all the reading and correspondence for the whole village, as very few people in those days could read and write. Josef first and his son Jacob followed him in this. They both held office in the county and Jacob had a son, Jacob Jr. who went on to be a State Senator for the district. In a letter from Germany it was stated that Jacob Jr. and Moritz were very religious, good workers, and smart. Jacob Jr. remained a Senator until the Hitler regime forced him out because he wouldn't become a Nazi He advised his children then to get jobs away from the farm so as to come under Social Security. They then became teachers and policemen, etc.

The children all grew up on this farm, getting as good a training and education as was available at this time. This family not only took an interest in animal husbandry, but also horticulture. This will be brought out later in their lives. It fell on Jacob, the eldest of the five children of Josef and Katherina to take over the farm and care for their parents in their old age. His wife's name was Anna. Walburga become of age and married George Siegle, born 26 April 1949, and died 6 June 1928. He was from the nearby village of Untercooken. He was a woodcutter for firewood and logs. After 25 years he became a foreman and took care of records and paid the workers. He worked 42 years in the wood business. He then became a cashier in the State Loan Office. They had two children, Jacob and Marie Weiland, born Siegel.

I must add something more here. George Siegel had a sister, Barbara who immigrated to America and went to Grand Rapids, Michigan. She met and married Frank Wagner and then moved to a farm 1 mile east and 1/3 mile south of Beal City, where their kin Frank Wagner now lives. This was about 1890. Information on the descendants of Barbara and Frank can be found in *"The Descendants of Joseph Siegel and Catherine Statsel"* by

Rev. Fr. Fox. They had many descendants in this area, Fussmans, Wagners, Foxes, and Simmers. I have garnered some information on Barbara from people who knew her, mostly Chris Fussman, my neighbor, now in his eighties. She was a very hard worker and did all the chores. She had varicose veins in her legs bad and they were swelled up and yet she would climb up in the haymow and mow away hay. She did everything. She always took a break at 10 a.m. and had ½ glass of wine, a slice of bread and a radish or onion. It was really good grape wine that she had made herself. She took of about two days a year and visited the neighbors, like Mrs. Reihl and Mrs. Kremsreiter, and others. She then had that done for the year and she could work, work, and work! She lived in the area most of her adult life and never seen Coldwater Lake. Chris remembers my Grandparents Moritz ad Mary visiting her with the horse and buggy, but never knew they were related. She was one of 16 children, most having died very young. Two of her brothers, Karl and Louis visited her occasionally. Chris remember they were very nervous and high strung and on the go constantly, walking real fast up and down the road. That was odd in those days.

My Aunt Leona Pasch remembers Barbara in her later years, sitting in a rocker on the front porch rocking away. She had a big bandage on her leg for years probably from the varicose veins. Josef Jr., the third child of Josef and Katherina found employment in Germany. I don't have much information on him. He did get married and had two children, Edward and Elizabeth, who immigrated to America settling in Defiance, Ohio.

The fourth child of Josef and Katherina was Johan "George" born about 1852 and the fifth child was my Grandfather Moritz born in 1854. Life was busy on the farm and from a young age the youngsters did what they could to make things go. In Northern Germany there was a more urban society, where they gradually worked into mining and manufacturing etc. Swabia, in the southwestern part of Germany was well suited for agriculture and forestry, as the Black Forest and much other forest land are in that area. We all know that good farmland and good forests go hand in hand.

Winters were moderate with usually much snowfall and it was difficult to get about in winter, so their houses were built accordingly. House-barns I call them, long sloping roofs with a good overhang, where they piled their firewood under the eaves. A loft over the house part for grain and a loft over the barn for hay. Having the animals inside then it didn't take much to heat, as the animals kept it quite warm with their body heat. These people then could spend the winter within the confines of their house-barn and not have to venture out for anything. The animal furnished the family with everything they needed. Eggs, milk, cheese, and meat to eat and leather for shoes on their feet, wool for clothes on their backs, heat for their house, soap to keep clean, and manure for the next year's crop. This has a lot to do with the Germans having a close association with animals. It is hard for us to imagine how important animals were to these people. Without the animals, they had nothing and were nothing.

In winter there was not much to do, but they did what they could, and this is how the area became famous for Coo-Coo-Clocks from the Black Forest area. They took to woodcarving and they discovered they could make these Coo-Coo-Clocks entirely out of wood. In the spring they would strap them on their backs and head for town where they would sell or trade them for seeds and the few things they would need to start the new season. To us they are a box hanging on a wall where a bird pops out and does his thing, but to an early Swabian, it was that and a whole lot more.

Here in America, my Grandparents wouldn't have had to "pick" beans during the winter. That is, put them through a belted machine similar to a sewing machine with a foot pedal to move the belt. As the belt conveyed the beans, the operator would "pick" out the bad ones. They could have taken them to Weidman and paid to have them picked as most other people did. Holmes Milling Company had a whole upper floor full of picking machines. But they did what they could through the winter to keep busy and earn a few extra bucks. Also, he had all clean beans and didn't have to take the miller's word for the "pick." Wise he was.

You would think that with these house-barns, there would be a lot of smell and the flies would be a bother, but it was no problem. I don't know why. Many farmers have signs out, "rooms for rent," much like motels in this country. While traveling there, we stayed at a number of them, real nice. We always got a light breakfast in the morning, usually hard-boiled eggs, hard rolls and coffee, real nice. The beds were odd, a real thick feather mattress on bottom and one thick cover blanket about eight inches thick on top. I think it was all goose feathers. It was just toast warm. Rural peasant life in Germany centers on the family and they in turn had a very close relationship with their village, which usually consisted of a Church, larger than the other structures about it. The burial ground was close by, the smithy, the mill, and perhaps an inn.

All things revolved about the husband and wife. The man was head of the household and all its enterprises. He controlled all, made the vital decisions, had charge of the field work and was the source of authority and discipline within the home. His wife was mother, her domain the house and all that went on in and about it. She was concerned with the garden and livestock, with domestic economy in its widest sense, the provision of food, shelter, and clothing for all.

So the women and children did all the chores, milked the cows, fed the chickens, and all. The man took care of his horse or horses and did the fieldwork and that's it. Well, Moritz wasn't any different than that. He had a few cattle but only 4 or 5 milk cows. Katie and Grandma always milked them, but not Grandpa. Come to think of it my Dad never milked any cows either, unless it was a fresh one that no one else could handle. He put the fear of the Lord into them.

It has been formulated that taking Germany in the last say 200 years, 25% of the people were peaceful citizens, and didn't want to bother anyone, a live and let live attitude. The other 75% then are what caused all the problems. Most Germans raised their sons to be soldiers. They were very militaristic and would follow their militaristic leaders anywhere to intimidate and gobble up their neighboring countries. They were always able to give the gullible world a sound reason for doing it. This of course led to two world wars, devastating Europe and leaving millions of causalities. The 25% of peaceful Germans then, being quite ineffective there, said to themselves, "enough is enough!" and immigrated to America. Some of them went to Argentina, Brazil and Canada, but most came here. Two wars took place in Germany while Moritz and his brothers and sister were growing up, The Danish Prussian War in 1864 and the France Prussian War in 1871. They were of war age, but they didn't cotton to this war business. Their father Josef died in January of 1872 and they started making plans to come to America. Their father had gotten letters from his brother Michael in Defiance, Ohio, saying that he was all settled and things were going well.

He said that he would sponsor the boys George and Moritz if they came, the time seemed right, get out before another war started. It took some time to get permission from the authorities to leave the country. Their brother Jacob was dabbling in politics some and this helped get the necessary forms signed. They scraped up all the money they could and were ready to go toward the end of July.

Each one packed their clothes in a suitcase. One church going change of clothes and one set of traveling clothes to change with what they were wearing, a heavy coat and a blanket. This suitcase was made to strap on their back. In a valise they packed their personal items, very important were cups, plates, and utensils. A few potatoes, sausages, hard-boiled eggs and bread enough for several days journey.

It was quite a process uprooting themselves psychologically, as well as, physically. Fears and anxieties were to be overcome. It was no easy task bidding their relatives and friends farewell. They all well knew they would probably never see them again.

Jacob and Josef took them with the horses and wagon a half days journey so they could be back by nightfall. Going west, hitching a ride when they could, they reached Stuttgart and boarded a train for the distance to the Rhine River where they boarded a riverboat. They were warned ahead of time of the dangers they would encounter. They had their money sewed into their belts and clothing that they would always keep on. They avoided talking to strangers and kept their mind to themselves. This traveling was all new to them and they rather enjoyed it, the bigger cities and all the activity on the river. They were now into wine country, which was new to them. At each stop of the steamboat they had to pay again to travel on. The further they went the more boat traffic was on the river. Rotterdam, the port city was bustling with thousands of people seeking passage on the steam ships to foreign shores. On arriving there were many ship salesmen, enticing them to travel on their lines, as it was a very competitive business. They paid them no mind, as they knew which line they were going on. Once there, the ship line had facilities where travelers could bathe while their clothes and luggage were disinfected. The emigrants were then examined by doctors and provided with inexpensive lodgings and food. The inspection routine seemed dehumanizing and they didn't like being poked, jabbed, washed, and sprayed. However, all the ship lines insisted on a strict procedure to avoid shipboard illness and avoid the added expense of returning emigrants to Europe in the event they were refused admission by inspectors in America.

Moritz and George accepted all this processing and were happy to be found in good health and mind and able to continue their journey. They brought enough food to last for most of the trip as food aboard ship was very expensive and it was mostly herring and potatoes. The ship companies supplied herring as it was nourishing and combated seasickness. They still had to buy some provisions on board, but not many. Each person received a daily ration of water and as the journey progressed, more and more vinegar was added to it to conceal the odor. It was a hard journey especially for families with children. Moritz and George fared well. They boarded ship on the 17th of August 1872 and steamed out on the 18th.

They left then, never to see again, that mysterious land across the ocean that all the older folks talked about when I was a kid, "The Old country." I didn't realize till I was older that this "Old Country" was a different place to each nationality, not just one "Old Country." No matter the nationality it was always a real place to me. The place they left for a better life. ...A place that would always be a part of them no matter how hard they tried to ignore it or dismiss it from their minds.

These emigrants on leaving Germany were preyed upon by con men and thieves. The boat trip was hazardous and frightening as you can image in 1872. Moritz and George and others on leaving that area and desiring safe passage, made a promise to send money back to build a chapel to their remembrance, which they did. Moritz sent 1200 marks, which was a lot of money then. The chapel is called the Saint Wendeline Chapel, and is between Walhausen and Beuron. It has a huge painting on the ceiling of a ship on the high seas. Our kinfolks in Germany told me of this, as we had no knowledge of it they look to it with great pride to this day.

They had a big celebration there in 1979, it being 100 years since being built. In the main speech that day, they talked of the people who had sent money to build it 100 years before. It was an uncomfortable voyage for emigrants like George and Moritz who didn't have much money and didn't know how much they would need later on. They were by nature conservative and like most of the immigrants were assigned to second class passage in steerage. Steerage referred the one or more below deck compartments of a ship located fore and aft where the ships steering equipment was located in an earlier era. They were no more than cargo holds, unpartitioned, and 6 to 8 feet high crammed with tiers of narrow metal bunks.

Travelers had to bring their own straw mattresses, which were cast overboard on the last day of the voyage. They cooked their own meals in small galleys shared by all those in steerage.

It was no consolation to these emigrants leaving Germany, but they were not the worst off. Among the Irish there were many that had not the paltry price of steerage, and once they got to Liverpool, the point of departure from England, there was no turning back. They had to find the means of a still cheaper crossing. From Canada came awkward ships built expressly to bring the tall timbers of American forests, lumbering vessels with great open holds not suited for the carriage of any westbound cargo. From Nova Scotia and New Foundland came fishing boats laden with the catch of the Great Bank, these craft also could be entrusted with no cargo of value on their return. Formerly both types went back in ballast, which is, they would pump in water for weight or ballast, to control the boat on the return voyage. Now they could bring the New World to the Irish. The pittance these poor creatures could pay- ten to twenty shillings was pure gain, and the ships had their ballast. As for the passengers, they could camp out in the empty stinking space below decks, spend an uneasy purgatory, preparatory to the redemption by America.

The shipping agents justified their case by saying that the Irish emigrant never knew what it was like to sleep in a bed. Give him pork and flour and you make the man sick. Let him lie on a good firm deck, eat salt herring and he'll be hale and hearty.

Throughout the hardships of the journey, Moritz and George, as did all the immigrants, began their readjustment in their lives. Living closely with people from different countries, having different customs and who worshiped God in different ways than they did, they began the slow and painful process of compromising some of their own values and customs to the demands of their environment. Far from the support of family and friends they began to wean themselves from the Old World even before they landed in the new. Moritz and George were quite educated compared to most of their fellow passengers and this afforded them an opportunity to keep busy and earn extra money. They did reading and writing for other passengers. Moritz was especially gifted in writing up legal type papers of all kinds, wills, rent agreements, buy or sell agreements, and so on.

Land was sighted on the 2nd of September and this created a great amount of excitement among the emigrants. They were still many miles from shore, but everyone crowded on deck for a view. It would be the next day before the ship docked, and few slept this night. As the sun rose on the 3rd of September 1872, the emigrants were awe-struck at the sights as the ship steamed through the narrows between Brooklyn and Staten Island, then up through Upper New York Bay. The great sight of the Statue of Liberty was denied my grandfather, as it wasn't built till several years later, being dedicated in October 1886.

Their boat steamed up through the mouth of the Hudson River about two miles and docked at the New

York City docks on Manhattan Island. The dock was chaotic, salesmen and shysters trying to sell clothes, food and anything, but they avoided them.

Moritz and George, as did all the passengers, had cleaned up and put on their best clothes to better impress the immigration officials. They had arrived in America but their journey wasn't over yet. Orders were shouted in many languages telling them what to do. They gathered their baggage and stumbled down the gangplank their legs now having to get used to land. On stepping on dry land they blessed themselves and murmured a prayer. A ferryboat was waiting to transfer them the two miles back down river to Castle Garden on the tip of Manhattan Island. This was the location of an old fort from the War of 1812, and it was made into the first immigrant processing center in America. It started operating in 1850, and was used until Ellis Island opened in 1890. Before 1850, they were processed on the boat docks, creating much difficulty in keeping records. With the amount of immigrants coming, a better system had to be found and they had to be protected from thieves and unscrupulous people, who would rob and trick them out of their money.

Here at Castle Garden, the immigrants were inspected, examined questioned, processed, and either admitted or rejected. The inspecting officials had ways of doing some tests without the emigrant knowing he was being tested. They had steps leading from the ferry dock to the main hall, and on carrying their luggage up the steps they would be observed for deformities and defective posture. On reaching the top the physicians could examine them under conditions of physical stress, such as produced by carrying luggage up a flight of stairs. Hands, eyes and throats were closely examined and the heart of the immigrant could be judged weak or strong by the luggage test. He was given an identification card written in his native language and was observed looking at it to check his eyesight. In bold letters was a message like, "scratch your right ear," or "look at your feet," or something like that. If he followed instructions it could be assumed he could read and was literate. Passing all their tests, George and Moritz were told that they could leave after having a full meal, the food being very good there. The officials were very helpful and they were advised of any problems lying ahead and they answered the many questions on the route to take to get to Defiance, Ohio. They re-boarded the ferry and went back up to the New York City docks. Having no reason to spend any time in New York, they booked passage on a river steamboat and went north up the Hudson River to Albany. They had never seen so much city in their lives, this America looked all city to them. In short time though, the city faded from view and they got their first look at American farm land, gently rolling with most of the crops harvested by now.

Passing through this farming area with the ferry stopping at all the small towns, they couldn't believe that they didn't have to share the boat with any farm animals, other than an occasional dog. In the Old Country they had to share the boat with goats, pigs, sheep, chickens, and anything else the farmers wanted to load on. They are so fond to give man and beast the same privileges. There were animals going to markets in New York by ferry but they had their own separate boat. Moritz and George thought that this American way made a lot more sense.

For its high bluffs stately passage and importance to industry the Hudson River has been called the Rhine of America. Albany was about 130 miles north of New York and on arriving there they were directed to take passage on the Western Canal for buffalo. The Mohawk River heads west from Albany and is known as the start of the old Erie Canal built in the years 1817-1825. Now it is known as the New York State Barge Canal. It is 363 miles long and they were told ahead of time that the fare would be two cents a mile. Travel here was by barge, or shallow draft boats. Horses walking on paths on each side of the canal pulled the barges.

This part of their journey was uneventful and accommodations along the way were good. Each night they stayed at way stations. Prices were reasonable and food was good but not much variety, usually corn meal or beans and tater soup, and always all the bread you wanted. The signs for the shops were very descriptive; usually a picture of what they sold, as many travelers couldn't read English. Buffalo was quite a thriving town but quite primitive compared to New York.

Here on Lake Erie they booked passage on a Great Lakes steamer and headed for Toledo, Ohio. They were happy they packed in a heavy coat, as it was quite chilly being toward the end of September. They were nearing the end of their journey and would soon be with their relatives and they felt rather secure. Lake Erie was a little rough but they paid no mind. At Toledo, they took passage on a ferryboat and headed up the Maumee River, Defiance was 60 miles up- stream. From the boat dock there they walked the four or five miles to Michael Weber's farm where they had a very happy reunion. Waterways have been a very important source of travel from medieval to modern times. But it just seems impossible to me that Moritz and George could travel from just a few miles from their village in Germany to the doorstep of Mike Weber in Defiance, Ohio, all by water, many different kinds of boats along the route, but all by water.

Chapter IV
THE LEARNING OF THE "AMERICAN WAY."

The winter of 1872-1873 was fairly mild and my Grandfather Moritz and his brother George did what they could around Uncle Mike's farm near Defiance in Noble co., Ohio. They earned their room and board and a little money to keep them going. They helped clear the land, cutting firewood and fence posts and pulling stumps. This sojourn in Ohio was really needed and good for them. Relatives and friends helped soften their transition from German emigrants to Americans. They had to learn English and living and working there, they picked it up rather quickly. Though all through their lives they were unable to shake that old German accent, few emigrants were able to. The reading and writing came slowly, requiring only time.

Their uncle, Mike Weber, had earned enough money to buy his farm by working in a copper mine in the Keweenaw Peninsula of Upper Michigan. That area was still going good but iron ore had been discovered in Negaunee and good jobs were available. Many different nationalities were working and living in harmony there.

That sounded good to Moritz and George. Come spring they boarded a barge on Maumee River headed for Toledo where they boarded a steamer for Marquette, again going all by water. Going through the Detroit River was interesting, as Detroit was a good size city, across Lake St. Clair and up the St. Clair River and out into Lake Huron. It seemed like they were out on the ocean again, but they could see land most of the time. In their other travels, they were amazed at the amount of forests in this country, but up to this point, a lot of land was being cleared for farming.

Going through the islands at the eastern end of the U.P. and in Lake Superior along the coast were endless forests, so much uninhabited land. It must have looked like the end of civilization to them. The locks of Sault Ste. Marie also impressed them. The Northwest Fur co. built the first lock on the Canadian side in 1797-1798. The American State canal, with locks was opened to traffic in 1855, which is the one their boat went through in that spring of 1873. I know those locks are sure fascinating to me, and we always watch the boats go through when we are in the area. Up through Whitefish Bay then and around Whitefish Point and out into vast Lake Superior, would they ever find their destination in such wilderness?

Marquette was a rowdy town with the boat docks and all the different nationalities working the copper, iron ore and coal mines. They stayed there a couple days and then took a coach the 12 miles inland to Negaunee. Like most small U.P. towns, the Finns lived on one end, the Swedes on the other, and a few Germans and Irish splattered in between and amongst. This area reminded them of the German landscape in the Old Country. Not mountainous but quite hilly.

The first discovery of iron ore in the Lake Superior region took place in the area of the city of Negaunee in 1844. The Carp River Forge was set up to melt and hammer down the ore but only operated nine years. With 30 mines in operation just in the city limits of Negaunee, there was just too much iron ore. Marquette was blessed with a deep and convenient harbor only 12 miles to the East. The raw ore was shipped by rail to the docks and loaded on boats bound for such cities as Cleveland for processing. Mr. Edward Breitung was the Mayor of Negaunee and a member of the Michigan House of Representatives of 1873. Mr. Breitung owned and operated a Hematite mine. Hematite is the chief ore of iron, occurring in crystals or a red earthy form. This mine was one of two Hematite mines in the Negaunee area and produced 1,728,976 tons of ore from 1870-1937.

They were hiring there and Moritz and George went right to work, and this suited them just fine. Moritz had an old saying that he lived and worked by: "Whatever is rightly done, however humble, is noble." This showed up in his work at the mine. He was punctual and he had respect for the tools he used. If a job wasn't quite done at quitting time, he stayed and saw that it was done and cleared up loose ends. Mr. Breitung supervised his mine personally and like any boss, was pleased when anyone come along to relieve him of some of his duties, someone who did them as good as if he would have done them himself. He recognized the qualities of trustworthiness, intelligence, and good personality. Moritz took on more and more responsibilities and always got the job done. In time, Mr. Breitung asked him to be his personal butler, and of course Moritz jumped at the chance. Both Moritz and George were here for one reason; to build up a grubstake enough to buy a plot of land in a German Catholic Community where they could settle down, farm, and raise a family. They were Swabians to the core. This opportunity then afforded better pay, clean working conditions, and free room and board in the big house on the hill, Mr. Breitung was a rich man. George continued to work in the mine, the work was all right but he didn't like the cold weather in winter. But until he could earn enough for his grubstake, he could put up with it. It was a lot better than the "Old Country." What he earned here was his to do with as he wished, and he saved most of it.

Moritz had a more pleasant disposition and didn't mind the cold weather. One thing he missed above all else was good apple cider. He liked beer too, and that would have to do till someday with the grace of God, he would have it all.

Another German family now bears some attention, as it is the family of Mary (Maria) Katherina Arens, the future wife of Moritz. When a German citizen wanted to leave there, he had to apply for a permit to emigrate. The following is an English translation of that document for Jacob Arens, father of Mary (Maria) Arens, my Grandmother.

Coblenz, June 10, 1868

The undersigned Kouigliche Government certifies that Jacob Arens, farmer, born 24 August 1830 in Munk, Mayen County applied for a permit to immigrate to America. Also for his wife Katherina born Steffens, on 26 May 1827, and the following children, under age and under his parental authority:

1. *Maria (Mary) Katherina Arens, born 29 Dec. 1858*
2. *Barbara Arens, born 26 July 1861*
3. *Peter Arens, born 12 June 1864*
4. *Gertrude Arens, born 27 April 1868*

And that the release from the Prussian citizen ship was granted. The release document annuls the Prussian citizenship for the above persons from the time it is handed over.

Kouigliche Prussian Regionary

Release Document

A.L. No. 1710

This was a very official looking document with a seal of the county seat and all. Coblenz is in west central Germany on the Rhine River. Jacob Arens and his family had visions of a better life in America. They left in June when they got their release, and arrived in New York 14 July 1868. That was four years before Moritz and George arrived. Mary K. was almost 10, Barbara was 7, Peter was 4, and Gertrude was 2 months old. That must have been a rough voyage coming across the Atlantic Ocean with a wife and four kids and one just 2 months old. They were poor and had to come in steerage.

Obviously the family that sponsored them lived in Fond du Lac, Wisconsin, as that's where they went first and they stayed there five years. I know they were farmers in Germany, but I don't know what he did in Wisconsin. To become a citizen of America, you had procedures to follow and it took several years. Jacob filed his "Declaration of Intent" to become a citizen in November of 1871 in Fond du Lac.

That five years in Fond du Lac gave him time to learn English and the ways of this country. I think Jacob and Katherina were fairly well educated as they both had a very good hand in writing. He must have been looking for a place to work and built up a grubstake as he moved to Negaunee, MI in 1873, arriving the same year as Moritz and George. These were hard working people and everyone did what they could. When Mary K became of age, she was 15 when moving there, she was looking for employment, which in those days was very limited for women. About the only work available were as housekeepers, maids for wealthy people, or dance hall girls. Yes, she hired on as a maid in Edward and Mary Breitun's big house on the hill, where Moritz was the butler. Both Moritz and Mary K had left the land, the "Old country" that offered them its rich heritage but little else. They left behind perhaps the chance to spend a lifetime as a low class tiller of someone else's soil, or the chance to wear a starched apron and move quietly about a carpeted drawing room in one of the big houses in Coblenz or

Berlin, serving tea to the ladies of high society. Behind every "Yes, Sir," or "Yes, Ma'am," there was the cold reality of knowing that you would never be one of them- not you, not your children, or your grandchildren.

So they left for this New World, believing that, if the streets were not, indeed, paved with gold that it was at least a place that cared more about what you were willing to do, than about the social class from which you had come. They were thrown together here by chance; the butler and the maid, the humble beginning of a new American Family that would fulfill their dreams of achieving as much as their ability and desire dictated.

Mary K did the general housework at the Breitung's. It was a big house and they didn't have vacuum cleaners or electric ovens or washing machines or running water, so there was much work to do. Permanent press was not invented and a really big chore was ironing clothes. Mr. Breitung was a professional person and had to dress well, so a lot of time was spent pressing clothes. Mrs. Mary Breitung did much of the cooking and Mary K learned much about running a household.

Moritz apparently did all the grocery and household shopping and he wrote down everything as to prices per pound or by the piece in a notebook. He brought all the ingredients for and made ginger pop, corn beer, lemon beer, and all kinds of things, the recipes were all in his book. The first part of the book he had English and German mixed, if he didn't know a word in English, he used German, but towards the back it was almost all English. He was learning.

Moritz and Mary K had quite a long courtship, but they wanted to earn enough money to have a good start in life together. They were married at 9 o'clock Tuesday morning 23 June 1885 in St. Paul's church, Negaunee. Mary was 26 and Moritz was 30 years old.

Being married now, the old Swabian instincts were stirring in Moritz, he had about enough money saved up to seriously think about his own little plot of the world where he could raise a family. There were many ads in the newspapers and magazines wanting settlers all over the Midwest and he didn't know where to go. In the winter of 1886-87, he journeyed to Montana. He came back and said it was so cold it froze the tails off cows. He didn't mind cold weather, but that was too much for him. Toward spring, he journeyed to Missouri where a German Catholic Community wanted settlers. He never seen so much rain, fog, and mud. Travel was about impossible except by train. He didn't like that at all. There must be a better place than that. Where he went in Missouri was around Hermann, west of St. Louis on the Missouri River, which is the center of Missouri's substantial German-American population.

Then an ad wanting settlers in a German Catholic community in Nottawa Township of Isabella County, Michigan, caught his eye. He took a train to Farwell, the nearest depot, and walked south to Beal City. Walking the few miles he wasn't impressed, pine stumps and scrub brush, it hasn't changed much! The closer he got to Beal, the better it looked. He stopped at VandeCar and did some inquiring, and then on to Beal City. Many German Catholics were moving in from the south-Westphalia, Pewamo, and Fowler. All good friend people and he partook of their hospitality.

The settling of any community is a story of many hardships and compromises and Beal city was no exception. The church had been built in 1882 and the people were justly proud of it. On the 8th of Dec. 1886, it burned to the ground. When Moritz got there in mid-summer of 1887, they were building a school house on the old church foundation to be used as a school and church, with plans to build a larger new brick church, which was completed in 1890. This brick church also burned to the ground in 1905. Moritz was impressed with the way these people carried on in the face of such adversity. They seemed to enjoy working and working together.

They didn't have a tavern in the area, but for sure they had something to "wet a whistle." Moritz got his first look at a "Michigan basement." …Never high enough to stand up in without stooping over with a dirt floor. It was a cool place under the house to store many things that in later years we would put in a refrigerator; butter, milk, taters, carrots, etc. It was also an excellent place to store a barrel of apple cider, the best cider that Moritz had ever tasted, and it was made from local grown apples. There was no doubt in his mind that he had found the spot in this world that was just right for him and his family.

THE WEBER FAMILY OF BEAL CITY MICHIGAN

After hiring a horse and buggy and looking at several parcels of land in the area, he bought 80 acres in Section 2 of Nottawa, that's one mile east and three miles north of Beal City on the N.E. corner of VandeCar and Denver roads. This parcel of land was two long forties. The north half he bought from Mr. Alonzo Frisbee and the south half along Denver Rd. from Levi VandeCar and wife. He finalized the deal on 8 August 1887. The town of VandeCar, which was at the corner of Weidman and VandeCar roads, and the road itself, was named after this Levi VanDeCar. Moritz made arrangements to rent the land for the next year. He thanked God for his good fortune, said good bye to his new friends, and headed back to Neguanee. His wife Mary K was with child at this time and he was anxious to get back and see that all was well. Katie was born 26 Dec. 1887. In 1888, they moved with the Breitungs to Marquette for unknown reasons and continued to work there for him till 1893.

Moritz must have presented a good picture of this area on getting back home because Mary K's father, Jacob Arens bought the 40 acres a half mile north of Beal where Chris Fussman now lives. He bought it from a woman named Laney Michels who lived in Negaunee. He paid $725.00 for it on the 24th of Feb. 1888. She only owned it one year and owed $500.00 on it. Apparently her husband died and she wanted out of it.

Moritz' brother George had worked all this time in the mines, and had saved up enough money to make his move. He was very sick of the cold weather, and as long as there was a warmer place in this country, he was going there. He headed out west and settled for a while in Nevada City, California, and later bought 26 acres of good land about a mile north of Rutherford in the Napa Valley wine country. This is Johan George Weber, he went by the name of George. Sometimes he signed his name J. George Weber...more on him later.

The years with the Breitungs were very good for Moritz and Mary K and they learned a lot that would help them later in life. It was difficult to leave, but in the spring of 1893, the Webers, with their daughter Katie left Marquette for Beal City. They were all on their own now, looking only forward to grasp all they could of the bounty of this great country. There was a house and barn on their property. The house, a two story patterned after most all the older houses in this area. They settled in and there was much work to be done. The barn was rather small but it would do fine for now. Horses and tools had to be purchased to start the spring work. They had to have cows for milk and butter, chickens for eggs and of course a chicken in the pot every Sunday was really living. There was a lean to sheep shed on the side of the barn, so he bought some "working stock" as most early settler did which refers to a block of sheep. Their job was to clean up new ground by eating grass, weeds, and brush, such as sumac, poison ivy, and black berry bushes. They would eat most anything and their wool was a good cash crop. When Moritz bought this land in 1887, he had rented it for the year 1888 to Theodore Faber. He must have come back here in July of 1889 and leased it for three years to David Wood; that timed it right for his permanent move here in the spring of 1893. This is the contract for the lease of the land to David Wood.

July 31, 1889

Know all men by these presents, that Moritz Weber of Nottawa Township, Isabella Co. Mich. Of the first part and David Wood of the same place of the second part, that Moritz Weber of the first part does hereby agree to lease seventy-nine acres of land to David Wood of the second part, for the term of three years from this date until Sept. 1, 1892 situated as follows, S ½ of the S.W. ¼ of the Sec. 2 town 15 N. range of 5 west. And the party of the second does hereby agree to pay all taxes accruing on said land for the time above stated, and also to clear and fence 8 acres of land, also clear brush off of meadow and move fence on line. If said party of the second fails to clear 3 acres per year, then the party of the first part shall have and hold one half of crops raised on said land for said year. The party of the second part has the privilege of clearing all the said 8 acres the first year, and to use the lumber now on place to keep fence and buildings in repair for said 3 years, and furthermore the party of the second part shall have one half of the crops now growing on said land for taking care of and harvesting the same.

Signed and delivered in   Signed:
Moritz Weber

Presence of Jesse H. Wood   Signed:
David Wood

I don't know how much of the land was cleared before Mr. Wood leased it. There probably was 15 or 20 acres and with the 8 acres he cleared, Moritz probably started out farming with about 25 or 30 acres of cleared land.

Moritz was doing now what he always dreamed of doing and he was good at it. He had a good background for farming in Germany, growing much on a small amount of land. He had also gained much self-confidence working for Mr. Breitung. Moritz was his own man and farmed his land primarily to provide for his family and then to make some extra money, which he did. He paid no mind to how his neighbors did things unless they were right. It didn't bother him a bit to do thing different and he always had time to keep his farm neat and his buildings in good repair. Moritz wasn't tight but he was frugal, paying attention to the little things and ways to make a few extra bucks on the things he sold. In all these things, his wife Mary K was able to do her share and more. She grumbled a lot about everything, but that' just the way she was and Moritz being a wise man, never let it interfere with progress. Moritz' interest and education in horticulture in Germany came into play here on this spot of the earth. His top priority was planting all kinds of fruit trees and shrubs…apple, plum, grapes, currants, blackberries, cherries, and many others, some just for the flowers. Mary was kept busy when the plantings started to bear fruit, and Moritz made his cider, beer, and wine. It seems odd for them to raise plum trees, but there is a reason. Plums are an old Swabian fruit with many uses; jams, sups, schnapps, puddings, wine, desserts, and they are good right off the tree. He was just following his old Swabian traits, or traditions. They made many improvements on this farm, clearing more land every year. Katie was getting old enough to pick up brush and roots and learn her way around the farm and how to work. She was a tireless worker all her life and always enjoyed it.

In 1898, Moritz and Mary K were blessed with the birth of a son, George. This was important to them as they were very much steeped in the old German tradition of turning everything over to the oldest son and he would keep his parents in their old age. I know very little about this George, my Dad's brother. He died at age 6 of unknown causes.

I want to give a brief history now of the other children of Jacob and Katherina Arens, the parents of my Grandmother. Their second child Barbara married one George Arneth. George and his brother Fred owned and operated a drugstore on Iron St. in Negaunee for many years. Most of that family moved to the Chicago/Milwaukee area where some of their kin still live. One of George and Barbara's daughters was named Martha. She was a schoolteacher and never married. She did a lot of traveling and visited here most every summer. She was quite racy and posed for many postcard pictures in Negaunee and Marquette. Postcards were very popular and the pictures usually said a lot more than the words on the back. Martha sent a lot of postcards during her summer travels to relatives here and many of them to Aunt Katie and Mary. She really rubbed it in to them about he travels, as she knew they didn't get off the farm that much.

The third of the Arens children was Peter. Peter was a bachelor and somewhat of a character. I think he was kind of an odd jobs guy in the U.P. When his folks moved here in about 1894 or so, he stayed up there for another 10 years or so. His mother died on 28 Aug. 1901 at the age of 74, and he might have come then to live with his dad.

Katherina was buried in St. Joseph's Cemetery here in Beal. Jacob died in 1913 at age 82. I don't know where he was buried, and I can't figure it out. Their farm a ½ mile N. of Beal was sold and proceeds, which were about all his assets were divided among their children. Peter then moved in with Moritz and Mary K. and lived there till he died in 1935 at the age of 71. He had strong feelings about his life in the Upper Peninsula, he liked it there and sometimes when he got disgruntled he would head back there. He had a long walk to Farwell and the train station. That long walk took enough time to settle him down. Grandpa Moritz would see him missing, hitch up the buggy and go to Farwell. Peter would be sitting at the depot, the train had already went through and he was ready to come back home.

All the older folks here remember him as he dug many graves at the cemetery, many times working at night by lantern light. He was paid $1.00 per grave. Peter never became a citizen and he had to register regularly as an alien. Gertrude, the youngest child of Jacob and Katherina, married Joseph Martin from this area and lived

THE WEBER FAMILY OF BEAL CITY MICHIGAN

2 miles N. of Beal and ¾ mile west. They must have got married about 1895 or so. They had two children, Jake Martin, a bachelor who worked as a hired hand on farms in the area, and Katie who married Lou Franz, a blacksmith from Weidman. Gertrude died before her dad in 1913, but I don't know for sure when. Katie and Lou Franz had a rough sledding, raising a family through the depression years, but most everyone was in the same boat. Lou was a tall, slim, good-natured fellow. His blacksmith shop was one block east and ½ block N. of the Methodist Church in Weidman.

    I just loved to go along with Dad to get things fixed there. He would heat the iron in his forge, and just make about anything you wanted, heat and hammer, heat and hammer. No such thing as a welder in those days, but he could bond iron together or make holes or bend it or just anything. When he was old and went out of business, I bought an old "Stover," one cylinder gas engine from him for $5.00, I still have it and it runs good. I have good memories of those relative, they were good honest hardworking citizens. Some of their kin live in the Weidman area today.

To a farmer who before had to pump water by hand, this creek was a Godsend. Some people had windmills to pump water but many didn't. Old Peter Tilmann, who owned our farm before we bought it, pumped water by hand for 5 or 6 cow, a few pigs, his chickens, and two horses up until about 1943 or so when he put in a pump jack with an electric motor. No wonder the son left home and said, "To hell with farming." One of their horses was name Jip and he never got enough water when they had to pump it by hand. When they pumped it with the electric motor, the horse got all he wanted and he stood right there and drank until he died…poor old Jip.

There was about as much cleared land on this 40 acres as on that 80 acres in Section 2 and it was better land. Now Moritz was kind of glad that his wife gave him a hard time about that long buggy ride to church. This was a much better deal, he liked it. This forty was Indian land owned by an Indian woman, Mary Chatfield, mother and sole heir of Norman Chatfield who was deceased. The warranty deed was signed on the second of February 1900. This warranty deed had to be presented to the U.S. Department of the Interior, Office of Indian Affairs for Approval. It was approved on 17 Oct. 1900. They paid $850.00 for this forty. I'm sure glad that Grandma raised a fuss about living up there in Section 2 or we would probably have our sawmill set up halfway to Woods Store someplace. This is much better. Apparently, Moritz made a deal with Mary Chatfield to build her a small house on one acre of this property in the NW corner, where Greg's house is. I have a quit claim deed dated 12 November

1903 which states that, for and in the sum of $35.00 it is hereby agreed that Moritz Weber is released from building a house for said Mary Chatfield. Boy, that was a cheap out, and he also got that acre of land back.

I don't know if Moritz and Mary moved that first year or not, I would say that they did. In 1903, Theodore Faber- he is the Grandfather of Art and Billy Faber and Irene Schmidt and that family- rented the 80 in Section 2. He had rented it also the first year Moritz had it in 1887. This is the rent agreement that Moritz drew up.

Know all men by these presents, that Moritz Weber of Nottawa Township, Isabella County, Mich. Of the First part and Theodore Faber of the Second part, that Moritz Weber of the first part does hereby agree to Lease eighty acres of land to Theodore Faber of the Second part for the term of from 15th day of April 1903. To the first day of April 1905, situated as follows: S ½ Of the SW ¼ of Sec. 2 town 15 N. Range of 5 West. And said party of the second part does hereby agree To plant 10 acres of wheat each year, the first year the Said party of the first part agrees to cut the wheat and Pay ½ of all the thresh bill, the said party of the second Part agrees to do the balance of the work the said Part y Of the second part agrees to harvest all the wheat the Second year and do all work and pay all expenses and Give 1/3 to the said party of the first part also the same 1/3 of oats, and potatoes and whatever may be raised each year. The said party of the second party agrees to harvest all hay and stack in shelter ½ of hay for the said party of the first part. The said party of the second part agrees to harvest all corn before the first *day of November each year and put 1/3 of corn in the crib and stack 1/3 of corn straw for he said party of the first part. The said party of the second part agrees to give all apples and plums on the north side, from the center of the house to the said party of the first part. The said party of the first part reserves a right to remove grape vines, currants, cherry trees, plum trees, blackberry vines, and shrubs as he feels disposed. The said party of the second part agrees to pasture four head of cattle and take care of them for the said party of the first part free of payment. The said party of the second party agrees to keep fences in repair, the said party of the first part got a right to get three loads of straw each year the balance of the straw got to be used on the place. The said party of the second part agrees to do two days road work and draw out all manure and put on the land described herein. The said party of the first part got a right to destroy Canada thistles and agrees to draw manure one day and Pick stones one day. The said party of the second part Agrees to pick the rest of the stones. The said party of the First part reserves roof and ceiling on the sheep shed which is on the south side of the stable. The said party of the Second part agrees not to plow more than one field where There was hay raised the year before, each year.*

Witness by: P. Yuncker   Moritz Weber

Sam Bierschbach   Theodore Faber

Mortiz and Mary owned the 80 in Section 2 for sixteen years before this contract with Theodore Faber was written and they lived there about 10 years. They sure made a lot of progress with fruit trees and shrubs and vines. He was good at that and now he was transplanting it to his new farm. When Mortiz and Mary made out this rent contract on 2 Nov. 1903, my Dad, Jacob Weber, was just a little over 2 weeks old. He was born the 14 Oct. 1903. His mother Mary was 45 years old and his Dad Moritz was 49 when he was born, they were just about running out of time. This turned out to be quite important to the family, as George died the next year in 1904. They had their share of hardships, but they overcame them. They were doing what they always dreamed of doing and were successful at it. I think better clear something up here. I maybe make it sound like Mortiz' wife Mary was a mean miserable woman. She really wasn't, she just liked to grumble a lot. You have to know how life was in those days. Men could get out and go places and do things, more of a variety. The women just did an awful lot of work and not much of it was easy. When there was nothing else to do, she could take a basket and pick up twigs in the woods. She was a good cook and always kept a neat clean house. And you know, along with milking cows and feeding calves and chickens, they always had a big garden and don't forget the "pickin'" beans; she was a busy woman. Maybe she had a reason to "bitch a little"…and also, like I've said before being a little discontent makes a lot of good progress.

Mortiz was becoming more familiar and acquainted in the Beal City area and in time he developed into the true character that he was. Moritz became an American citizen on 19 February 1914 in Mt. Pleasant, number 291059. Voting rights and being active in church and community affairs were very important to Moritz and his family. He served as Nottawa Twp. Treasurer from 1908-1912. He had a loud high-pitched voice and in church he sang loud and about two notes behind everyone else. The rosary and a lot of other prayers were said in German and on ending a Hail Mary or Our Father, he always had 2 more words to say when everyone else was done. He never really rushed into anything, but he always got the job done and done right.

One day he was broadcasting clover seed in the field next to the road and it was a little windy. He was sowing and singing at the top of his lungs. A neighbor came walking along the road on his way to Beal to get a can of kerosene and hollered across the fence, "Moritz, it's too windy to sow clover seed."

Moritz took right off across the field sowing and singing, "As long as it stays in the field, tra la, tra la, tra la." I can remember Dad saying that phrase and if you are around Fuzz much, sooner or later you will hear him come out with that old family jewel- "As long as it stays in the field," and we all know, it's a so-what, I'm doing it situation.

Moritz was in his fifties about this time and was used to a slower pace of life, working with horses and all and was slow to see the merits of the automobile, as most people were. He was helping his brother-in-law, Peter Arens, drag the field along the road on the Chris Fussman place which they owned. A car came along and backfired a time or two, probably on purpose, and the horses bucked and tipped the drag over. He yelled after the car, "If you can't afford a horse, you shouldn't be on the road!"

Allie Schumacher who lived across the section to the east, tells of hearing Moritz talking to his horses on clear days. The horse's names were Maggie and Dollie and he talked to them constantly as he worked. He would say, "Maggie Dollie, Maggie Dollie," and then say a whole bunch of German, which he preferred, and sometimes mix in some English. This was a kick back to his early German life where the people had a very close relationship with their animals, and he talked to them in an almost human way. All the old folks talked a lot of German and my folks did too when they didn't want us kids to know what was going on.

Moritz was troubled by stomach pains, maybe it was ulcers or something. He was told that the only cure was a warmer and dryer climate. He took a train and headed west to scout it out. At Kansas City he was bunked with a gentleman who was going out west also. Moritz was telling him about his ailments and this traveler told him to take a quantity of peroxide, full strength and it would cure his affliction. At the next stop, he got off the train, went to a drugstore and purchased a bottle of peroxide and took a dose right then. He got back on the train and when he got to Denver, he felt so good, he turned around and came back. As far as I know, he didn't have any more stomach problems.

Things had settled down and going good, it was time to follow his dream farther. In 1907, they purchased an 80 acre of land from one John Anthony Neyer, which was across the road to the south, it was the N ½ of the NW ¼ of Section 22 of Nottawa Township. That's where Weber Brothers Sawmill is now. This is known then as "the Old Homestead," and Moritz's pride and joy. The house was a two story or actually it is the south part of Jeff and Sue's house. This was Moritz and Mary's last land purchase and their last move till they moved back across the road to Section 15 when my parents Jake and Eleanor married in 1926. There was an old shack of a barn on the place about half way between the present barn and the road, just north of the house.

The "Old Homestead" Moritz Weber bought was the original 1882 home of Jackob and Frances Neyer, shown left with son Jacob "Jake-" Neyer.

Photo courtesy John F. "Jack" Neyer, Mt. Pleasant MI, who is Jackob Neyer's great-grandson and Jacob "Jake" Neyer's grandson son.

When Moritz first bought that 80 in Section 2 and moved down from the U.P., he had found the good German Catholic community to raise his family and till the soil, his dream since arriving in America. This was his first step and through their family efforts, the bounty of their plot of this earth did them well. The buildings were in good condition and served them well without much extra work. And it was free of debt.

The Weber's second move buying the 40 acres in Section 15 was a better location and definitely a good move. The buildings were better than the last place, the barn was bigger and with the creek close by, that was nice. The house was more than adequate for his growing family. He had all kinds of fruit trees and of course, apple trees for apple cider. With all this, what more could a man want?

The progress thus far of this German immigrant family was all they ever hoped to attain and more. But now the question arose, "What heights can be attained in this new country by immigrants arriving on these shores with little but the clothes on their back and a vision of things better?"

This new country operated differently than the "Old Country." You got to either keep or sell whatever you produced. The government officials didn't come and take 3 pigs and leave you with one or take one horse and leave you with one or take most of your grain and leave you with barely enough to get you through the next winter and enough to plant in the spring. Things were sure different here. Oh, sure, you had to pay a little tax, but you could get the best deal.

This "Old Homestead," then was going to be everything beyond what they ever thought they would accomplish. This would be their monument, and it was.

The 80 acres in Section 22 the "Nottawa Center Farm," with its tumble down barn, rickety fences, and a rundown house would be starting from scratch on raw land just what Moritz wanted-the ultimate challenge. On the 30 January 1907, Moritz and Mary K sold the 80 in Section 2 to Peter and Anna Smith. It had served its purpose and now with plans for this next step the money from the sale could be put to good use. Peter and Anna owned that 80 up until about 1944 or so, then Julius Martin and his wife Amelia- that was Uncle Ernie Schmidt's sister- owned it and maybe it had another owner. Now it is owned by Vogel Farms, Bill and Ken. It is all cleared; it looks like fair land. It is fairly flat and all slopes to the east. Whenever I pass by that place I visualize my Grandfather out there planting fruit trees and shrubs, or cutting brush and trees to make more farm land.

John Anthony Neyer, who owned the 80 acres in Section 22, lived in Chicago and it took awhile to get this deal made. There were many letters back and forth. This John Anthony Neyer, who went by the name of Tony, was an artist in painting and woodcarving. He had lived in the house on the 80 acres. It was a 2 story, which is the South part of the Weber homestead. He sold paintings door to door in the area. He made an intricately carved wooden

Crucifix which hung over the upstairs stairway in the house. The family then went back to Austria for 10 years, leaving the Crucifix behind in the house. On returning to America, they settled in Chicago and sold the farm to Moritz. About 1970 the house was rented out and the Crucifix was taken down and I stored it away.

In our Farm Centennial year 2000, Gregory refinished and painted the cross and cleaned the sculpture and it is displayed in the Weber Beal City Museum. During our Farm Centennial celebration, descendants of the artist Tony Neyer went through the display asked my son Jeff about the Crucifix. He told them about it handing in the house and that's all we know about it. They then told him the history of it. These descendants were Julie (Quillen) Gross, Barbara (Quillen) Crandall, Beth (Quillen) Judge, and Heidi Quillen. These ladies mother is Hedy (Neyer) Quillen who along with her sister Agnes (Neyer) Engler are nieces of the artist Tony Neyer. Also, this Tony was Governor John Engler's great uncle. It is truly amazing how stuff like this gets down through the generations and now it will live on. I think the Crucifix had something to do with it. A bit of trivia: Tony had paintings displayed in the Chicago Museum of Art and Agnes Engler has a copy of one of his paintings in her living room, it's beautiful.

The deed on this sawmill 80 was signed on 23 April 1907. I don't know how much they paid for it. They paid $1000.00 as down payment the middle of February, but beyond that I don't know, maybe 2 or 3 thousand I would guess. Although, the buildings weren't much and it was run down, maybe they paid only about $1500.00 or so.

Moritz loved this new place with its broken down fences and all, he would build it up just the way he wanted it. He started out with a big round roofed barn. He was doing as all German farmers did whenever they settled. They build their barn first and take care of their animals, and when all is on sound footing, then look at the house. This new barn was to be timber frame construction with wooden pegs to hold it together. It was completed the last of July. A steam engine and thrashing machines was passing by on the road and a spark from the engine ignited a straw stack by the old barn about half way from the road to the new barn. There was a westerly breeze and in no time sparks from the straw stack had ignited the new barn and the whole business went up in flames.

Perhaps the greatest earthly fear that people in those days had was fire. They were about completely helpless once a fire got started well. They did have some ways to ward off fire though, they prayed, and during bad lightning storms they would burn palms in their stoves. You know, blessed Palms, like you get in church on Palm Sunday. During a very bad storm when my Dad was small and his mother was putting some palms in the stove, there was a really big flash of lightning and a clap of thunder that shook the whole house. The fear was very evident in everyone and my Dad was terrified. He ran up to his Ma, gave her a kick as high up as he could and hollered, "More palms! More palms!" He thought if a little did some good a whole bunch would do wonders. And really there was very little they could do, except pray. There were no fire engines and you couldn't get close with a bucket of water, just try to save any other buildings was about.

This fear of fire stayed with these old folks till they died. When Aunt Katie was getting older and living alone, the folks would send us kids over to check on her on cold days. The windier and colder it got, the less fire she had in the stove, and she would just put on more clothes.

So the barn was all burned up. It was insured and they had learned a lot and the basement walls were still good. They went right to building another one. Moritz realized that they didn't have time before fall to square up all those timbers and make all those mortises and tendons and drill all those holes for pegs, and mainly, the logs weren't even cut yet. The other barn was all planned out ahead, the logs had been cut the previous winter and in the spring and early summer the frame was prepared and ready for the "Barn Raising." All the neighbors and members in the community helped on these barn raisings with several of them being built each summer. It was a good excuse to get together, work together, and socialize. The first Saturday night after the barn was done they had a "Barn dance" on the new barn floor. A fiddler would be a playing' and all would dance and of course a few guys would do the jig, it just took a little hard cider.

This new barn would be all laminated plank frame as it stands today. Moritz went to Weidman and purchased all the planks and the shiplap for siding and wood shingles from the Holmes Milling company lumberyard. Some logs had to be cut for the floor beams, when that was done it went up fast and they were ready for winter. In the next couple years they built four more buildings. A wood shed just to the east of house and a little south. This was about 18x20 ft. or so. A combination chicken coop and corncrib with a drive in the center was built to the east of the wood shed and a little north, this had an "A" shaped roof. Directly east of that was an identical building used for a garage and for storage. These two buildings were where the three story chicken house stands now. My Dad and others tell of the discontent of my Grandmother Mary Arens Weber. She was always grumbling about her place in life and made life a little miserable for the family.

In those days the farmers didn't put all their eggs in one basket. They raised horses, cows, chickens, pig, and sheep, along with many different kinds of crops for their own use and to sell. Beans were a good cash crop and through the winter the women folk would "pick" the beans. The good beans went to Holmes Milling Co. of Weidman to sell, and the "pick" beans or "cull" beans were used as hog feed. Most every farm had what they called a "Cook house" with a big iron kettle to cook the beans. This was the fourth out building that Moritz built, although it might have been the 1st one finished. About 16x20 feet with an "A" roof, it was in a line with the east end of the barn, south, midway between the barn and the garage and storage building. The kettle was built into a cement base where fire could be built underneath and a brick chimney up the back. This was a nice warm place and my Dad said whenever Grandma got to raising a fuss in the house, Grandpa and he would head out to cook beans. They spent many winter days out there even if there were no beans to cook. I remember that our "old cook house" was there till it tumbled down even though we hadn't used it for years. Looking back, I think Dad had a lot of old memories of it with Grandpa and all, and he couldn't see it go. The bean kettle was on the north end and a workbench was built along the south wall with a row of windows above it. The bench had a big wooden vice mounted on it and this made a good well lit place to whittle out neck yokes single trees, and wagon tongues.

Dad raised a lot of hogs and we cooked many beans for them. Those hogs liked a nice warm meal on cold winter days and they did well on them when fed along with ground grain. I loved the smell of them beans cooking'. That cookhouse completed the buildings except for the sheep shed on the NE corner of the barn it wasn't attached to the barn but was right up to it. My Dad used it was a hog barn with machinery storage above and later when we got into chickens, it was full of them. One of the first things Moritz did on getting this farm was plant a big apple orchard with many different varieties of trees. It covered about 2 or 3 acres and was directly east of the cookhouse, garage, and storage shed. He wanted to be sure he had plenty of apples for cider, which he loved. Our shop building is on part of this orchard area. His plum trees and pear trees, berries and vines were just north of the house in the garden area.

Okay, now the out buildings were fine, but the house wasn't so good. Better do something with that.

They built a single story addition onto the north side of the old house with a full basement. They put a new roof on the whole thing and new siding. They had a nice porch out the front and back too. They put a good coat of paint on all the buildings. The house rebuilding was done in 1909 or 1910 and remained the same till 1922 when they built the upstairs on the north part of the house; in other words they raised the roof.

This place 1910 was indeed a showplace and a monument to these immigrants who started out with nothing but the clothes on their backs and a dream. This is and I hope always will be "The Weber Homestead." In all the endeavors of Moritz Weber and all German settles, they set a pattern that was distinctly different from other nationalities that settled our nation. His peculiarities of speech and customs made him distinct from the other colonial types, but his individuality was marked by far more noteworthy traits of character. Mr. Benjamin Rush, a noted Philadelphia physician, a signer of the Declaration of Independence, member of Congress, Treasurer of the U.S. Mint and a distinguished essayist on medical, social, and literary topics, was a keen observer of the success of the German immigrant. He wrote an essay giving 14 points of how the German farmers differ from most of the other farmers in an area.

In condensed form here are the 14 points:
1. *In settling a tract of land the Germans always provide large and suitable accommodations for their horses and cattle, before they lay out much money in building a house for themselves. His*

sleek and well-fed cattle were a source of the greatest pride to him. The housing of them brought far better results than leaving them to run wild.
2. *They always prefer good land or that land which has a large quantity of meadow ground. By attention to the cultivation of grass, they often grow rich on farms on which their predecessors have nearly starved. The Germans also quite commonly occupied wooded-land, they knew that where there was rich forest growth, good soil was to be found underneath.*
3. *In clearing new land, they cut the trees and either used the lumber or burned them to have the land cleared in one year and ready for farming.*
4. *They feed their horses and cows well, thereby practicing economy, for such animals perform twice the labor or give twice the yield of the less well fed.*
5. *The fences of German farms are generally high and well built, so his fields seldom suffer from the inroads of his own or his neighbor's animals. Also there was no scarcity of wood but scarcity of labor to watch cattle.*
6. *The German farmers are great economists of their wood. They do not waste it in large fireplaces, but burn it in stoves, using one fourth as much wood and the house is more comfortable, thus saving much labor and time cutting wood. They had their stove in the middle*

of the room so the family could be equally warm rather than burning their faces and freezing their backs before a fireplace. Also, the habits of industry were encouraged like spinning, weaving, and sewing, by being comfortable.

7. *They keep their animals warm as possible in winter to save feed, for cold animals eat much more than when they are comfortable.*
8. *The Germans live frugally in their homes in regard to diet, furniture, and dress. They sell the more profitable grain such as wheat and eat the rye and corn. They use few distilled spirits as whiskey and rum, preferring cider, beer, wine and simple water. They are afraid of debt, and seldom purchase anything without paying for it.*
9. *Kitchen gardening the Germans introduced altogether. They had useful vegetables for every season of the year. This was important in preventing diseases of the skin. All Germans had a good knowledge of horticulture and along with vegetables, had orchards in abundance.*
10. *The Germans seldom hire men to work on their farms. The wives and daughters frequently helped during the busy times.*
11. *The Germans expressed much joy on the birth of children, and they produced kin their children not only the habits of labor but also a love of it.*
12. *The Germans set a great value upon patrimonial property, that is, keeping the land in the family, this makes an estate a matter of family pride.*

> 13. *The German farmers are very much influential in planting and pruning trees, also in sowing and reaping, by the age and appearances of the moon. Of course this was a matter of superstition, but it resulted in giving close attention to the climate of the country and therefore was an aid to success. It wasn't all bunk, we still rely on the divining rod to find water and if you butcher a hog at the wrong time you don't get much lard.*
> 14. *The German farm may be distinguished by the superior size of their barns, the plain but compact form of their houses, their good fences, the extent of their orchards, the fertility of their fields and meadows, all of which have the general appearance of plenty and neatness in everything that belongs to them.*

You can see Moritz in all of this; he was a good steward of all that the Lord provided for his use. One of Moritz's old proverbs: "God will provide the vittles, but He will not cook the dinner." It is interesting to note the relationships of the immigrants to their villages in Germany and the importance of each man and his place in the village, this made a successful village as such. It didn't work in this country of free enterprise. The traits that made a bad member of a village there were traits that succeeded in the new world.

You could be your own man here.

THE WEBER FAMILY OF BEAL CITY MICHIGAN

Sidebar:
THE BLESSING OF THE WEBER 1 WELL
By Jack R. Westbrook

The Jacob Weber #1 drilling attempt to find oil beneath the Weber farm was issued State of Michigan Drilling Permit No. 2377 to W. J. Bernier of Nottawa Oil and Gas Co. Clare, Michigan, *during the week of March 6 to March 9, 1935, by the then Michigan Conservation Department.*

Drilling commenced on April 12, 1935 and, to add an additional twist for luck, the pastor of St. Philomena's Catholic Church of Beal City, Father Zugelder *(right in photo on previous page)* was invited to the site for luck and an unofficial blessing.

Nonetheless, the well reached total depth April 21, 1935, at the top of the white Marshall Sandstone, and was declared a dry hole.

Chapter VI
CALIFORNIA GOLD

When I first started researching this Weber Family Genealogy, to say I was confused would be a gross understatement. Many favorite family names come down generation after generation and also in each branch of the family. We have many Jacobs, Ohans or Johns, Josephs, Katherinas – spelled three different ways, Marys, Maries, and what caused me so much confusion was the Georges. There was George Seigle in Germany married Walburga my Grandpa's sister, and George Arnneth in Negaunee married Barbara Arens, and George Weber in Midland from the other branch of the family, my dad Jacob's brother George and 3 George's in Defiance, Ohio, and my Grandfather Moritz's brother John-George Weber, which was his legal name. Sometimes it was J. George Weber, but mostly it was just George. He immigrated to America with Moritz, worked in an iron mine with Moritz and when he got sick of the cold weather and had enough money, he settled in California. I did not know he existed until I got well into this history. This is his story.

My maiden Aunt Katie, my dad's sister, born in Negaunee in 1887, moved with her parents to Nottawa township in 1893, first in Section 2 and then to what we call "Katie's forty" in Section 15. They moved to the Weber homestead in Section 22, one mile north of Beal City in 1907. When Jake and Eleanor were married in

1926, Katie and the old folks moved back across Weidman road to "Katie's Forty," where she lived the rest of her life. She tended her parents Mortiz and Mary in their old age. Moritz died in 1928 at age 74, Mary died in 1942 at age 84.

Katie had a lot of traits associated with her earlier life with emigrant German parents, more so than my father as she was born in 1887 and by the time Jacob was born in 1903, they were a lot more Americanized. Her way of eating was as all Germans eat. While cutting off a piece of meat to eat she would hold her fork backwards in her left hand and stab the small portion she was cutting off and then, while still holding her knife in her right hand, she would put the meat in her mouth with her fork still backwards or upside down. While we hold the big piece of meat with a fork, cut off the portion we want to eat, lay our knife down, change our fork from our left hand to our right, stab the portion and put it in our mouths with the fork in the upright position. A lot of eating was done with a knife, which was always held upright in the right hand when not being used. The knife was also used a lot for pushing food onto the fork, while we use our finger. Table manners called for resting the wrist, the wrist of the knife holding hand on the table's edge while eating with the other hand. This goes back to a time when it was thought wise to keep both hands in plain sight, particularly when one held the knife. Us kids used to try that and always got scolded for it. In Germany, many people do it Katie's way to this day.

During World War II, an American Pilot was shot down over France. He landed with his parachute and the French underground found him and tried to sneak him across the border to safety. During the journey, they stopped to eat in a café. He cut up his food with his knife and then picked up the fork in his right hand to eat. This identified him as an American and he was captured by the Germans and spent the rest of the war in a prison camp.

My Grandparents didn't live in the Upper Peninsula all that long, but something they picked up from the Finnlanders was different. While drinking hot coffee, they would pour a quantity into their saucer and then kind of slurp it up, all the while blowing on it to cool it, repeating the process as needed. And if they liked sweet coffee, they would drop a few sugar cubes in the saucer and slurp the coffee through the cubes as they floated to their mouths. A lot of this puts me in mind of how "Hagar the Horrible" would do it.

Katie was hard working and industrious, never letting anything go to waste. She raised a big garden with many flowers, which she loved and took great pride in. Along with not wasting anything, she saved everything, not throwing anything away. My wife Shirley says I'm the same way. She saved all her old magazines, receipts, bills, patterns, clippings from newspapers that might be of interest later on, buttons, old lace, hat pins, and so on. What I am forever grateful to her for is, she saved all the letters and postcards from friends and relatives wherever they were. In those days it was the only to communicate without going in person. A big thing in those days was postcards, which they called "postals." Some she saved were those I took to Germany and with them located my kinfolk living there. I hadn't paid much attention to these old letters, tied in bundles with string, until I started researching this family history business and besides, I couldn't find anyone to translate them anyway, all old German.

One day a gentleman, Fred Wiesener from Mt. Pleasant came to the Sawmill for some lumber. He talked a broken- English and I asked him what nationality he was. He said he was born in Germany and came here at age 20 he was about 50 or 55 years old. We visited awhile and I asked him about these letters I had and if he could translate them. He said he had had this old German up to the third grade in school at which time the government decreed that only the new or high-German would be used and taught in schools. He thought he could help out and in the fall we could get started. The postmarks started in late 1918 and ended about 1930. I wondered about that, why this time span, not knowing what was to come.

The First World War started in 1914 and ended in November 1918. America was in that War with England and France against Germany. My dad was just too young for that war, but many from this area went to "Fight the Kaiser." For Americans of German descent it meant fighting many close relatives. Albert Hundt, who married my Dad's sister Mary, was in that war. There was no correspondence possible during the War and the letters started right after.

The letters were from Moritz Weber's sister, brothers, and nephews in Germany. They tell of the War being now over and they had a miserable time of it. The government took in all the Gold and silver and gave the people Marks, which is German money and it became worth less and less. Most of their livestock went to France as war reparations, along with much money. The Englishmen took all the mature timber back to England. The Jews controlled the goods of the Country and as they were traders and shopkeepers, they charged sinful amounts for everything, only the rich could afford it. The Jews then sent their wealth to America. This then started the Germans hatred of the Jews. In ten days, 16 November to 26 November 1919 the Frank went from 5 Marks to one American dollar to 20 to 1, and it got worse as time passed. Everything was rationed. Anything they do get comes from America, for which they are grateful.

The letters go on about the war and how miserable the country is because of the war and they would go on about getting some money from America to Germany and some business about power of attorney and I don't know what all. One letter said they had had some friends in New York who were coming back to Germany and maybe Moritz could give them the money and get it to them without the Government getting a cut of it. We couldn't figure out what they were talking about. It was like walking in on the middle of a play. I told Fred, we are getting nowhere, let us try this small packet of letters which like the others were tied with string and on the top envelope someone had written in English, "Letter's from

George." The postmarks started in 1904 and came from St. Helena, California, and all written in German.

This of course was my Grandfather Moritz's brother George alias Johan George or J. George. Up to this time I didn't know Moritz had a brother. I did know that there was a "missing link George" out there someplace. At times, I thought it might be Dad's brother George, but that didn't add up as he died at age 6. No one in the family had ever said anything about California George that I could remember. Somehow though I just knew he existed. I had gone to Midland to check out the relatives there. His name was George Weber, but I just knew that he wasn't the person I was looking for. However, that visit to Midland prompted a daughter, Louise Schick to contact me 15 years after I was there and got that family branch figured out which I covered earlier in Chapter 3. Some postals I had were from Edward and Elizabeth Weber from Defiance, Ohio, and they called Moritz, "Uncle," I thought ho is this? I went to Defiance, Ohio, about 1985 to check things out. I went to one Albert Weber's home, he didn't have much interest in this genealogy business, but he did direct me to one older lady of the Weber clan, but I didn't learn much. I did enjoy my visit with them though. This one lady Mrs. Beaver seemed to know a lot about the seedier side of the Defiance Webers. She would say "I really shouldn't be telling you this," but she always did. She did give me a copy of a new item of the celebration of Michael and Orttilia's 50th Wedding Anniversary. It had a listing of all their children and grandchildren who gave me the information I needed to tie in the Midland Weber's to them. It was a worthwhile trip. After this run to Defiance, I had given up all hope of ever uncovering anything on this elusive relative George. On reading these letters from California then, right away he starts calling Moritz his brother, which he was. At last, the "missing link!"

While Moritz was searching the Midwest for a place to settle, George went to California. He wanted a place with a warm climate. In one letter he writes, *"Yes you can believe me, I would have loved to live there as your neighbor in my old age, if it wasn't for the snow. I wouldn't like to go back where snow is, it's cold enough here at night."* George settled first in Nevada City, California, about 80 miles West of Reno, Nevada.

The discovery of gold in California led to the greatest mass adventure since the crusades. Ironically, we owe that first gold strike to the Forest Products Industry. When John A. Sutter needed a saw mill to provide lumber for his growing empire in the Central Valley, he sent James Marshall to seek out a spot on the South Fork of the American River. After some searching, Marshall found a site with tall stands of pine and plenty of water to drive the hill. During routine inspection of the gray-pine sawmill early in the morning of January 24, 1848, Marshall also found gold. Sutter's mill changed history. The town of Bodie was in this "Mother Lode area." It was one of the toughest and most lawless mining camps in the west, at its rip-roaring peak in 1879. A lot of miners in the Upper Peninsula of Michigan that were sick of the cold weather and snow said, "By God I'm going to Bodie." A famous line is attributed to a young lady who wrote in her diary, "Goodbye God, I'm going to Bodie." Bodie at its peak had 10,000 people, as did many gold towns. It's not on any maps today. It is a ghost town and was located just north of Mono Lake.

Nevada City where George went in the early 1890's was the "Mother Lode" gold area and was probably about the same as Bodie, as were many gold mining towns. I don't know if he worked mining gold or what he did. I know he was a God-fearing Christian, it was probably too sinful of a place for him and he moved on. Maybe he thought he could get his "gold" in the California wine country.

If he left the Upper Peninsula of Michigan about the same time as Moritz in 1893, he was in Nevada City about 10 years. In the fall of 1903, he purchased 26 acres of land in Napa Valley, 3 miles south of St. Helena or one mile North of Rutherford. He paid $4,500.00 for it, $3,000.00 in cash and he got a loan of $1,500.00 at 8% interest from the bank of St. Helena, where he bought the land and he still had $575.00 cash in the bank. All this information on George is from his letters. There is a 2-story house on the property and he rents a part to an English couple for $8.00 a month. The land is flat and good in the middle of the valley, one-mile east and one-mile west of his place. Beyond that begins the foothills. The county road and the railroad go past his property. Swabians by nature are proud of these possessions as signs of what you are. George liked his place and was proud of it, he writes, "there is cheaper land to be hand, but it is not so good, so

I didn't want it." This small valley is supposed to grow the grapes for the best wine in America. They also raise plums, prunes, walnuts, almonds, corn, and a lot of hay. You can grow most anything there, just plant and maybe water it a little. He plans on planting 6 acres of grapes, as they will bring $15.00 to $18.00 a ton. He had 19 apple trees and 5 large oak trees. He raised hay on the rest of his land and between the rows of grapes, he gets $10.00 a ton for the hay. George tried to entice Moritz to come to California to settle. He tells of his neighbor who was from Kansas City and wants to go back there. He paid $8,000.00 for his place but a man can make it good for $3,000.00 or $4,000.00. As the letters move along he only talks of his crops and the prices and weather-too dry, too wet, or too much dry wind, etc. After several letters I said to Fred, "this guy must have been a bachelor, as he never talks of any family members or anything related to it." He has little interest outside of his farming, prices of crops, and weather.

Apparently, he was the Godfather of my Dad's brother George who died at age 6. In 1904, he enclosed a 25-cent stamp for George's Easter eggs and at Christmas time he sent $1.00 paper money for George's Christmas gift.

In 1905, they put an electric trolley past his place along with the railroad and county road. In 1906, he writes about the San Francisco earthquake. Thirty million gallons of wine was lost by fire. The worst of the quake was the fires. Grapes, then, were a real good crop, bringing $27.00 to $30.00 a ton. The only damage he had was the two chimneys on his house broke off over the roof. He writes often "*I wish we could get together.*" Now his grapes are four years old and he is harvesting a good crop. In 1912, Uncle Sam put on an 8-cent a gallon wine tax, he is very unhappy with this.

In 1915, he seems to be changing his tune about California. He writes, "If you plan to live in California, better come first and look because a lot of people don't stay, but it's up to you. You can't make cider from California apples as the juices are too weak." In fact, I think he was being very discouraging as he knew Moritz loved this apple cider and he wasn't about to move where he couldn't have it.

George must have been a kind of horticulturist, as Moritz must have wrote him about his trouble with a crop of potatoes. George writes back:

"Dear Brother and family,

The potatoes are maybe lying too thick on top of one another, or they are getting no air, or have been in too wet. Maybe the ground is not good for potatoes, but also, there are years when potatoes just rot."

In the next letter he says he will send the potatoes next week. He must have sent Moritz a new strain from there, thinking that might help. All of George's letters end like this:

"I am, thank god, healthy and wish with all my heart that these writings will find you the same way. Many regards to all, George."

When translating the letters from 1914-1915, I remarked to Fred that George seemed to be getting a little senile and shaky and being alone out there he appeared to be getting lonesome, and then it hit us both at the same instant! That money the relatives in Germany were talking about! George must have died leaving his estate to his brother and sister. Then everything added up and we went back and reread the letters from Germany and they made a lot more sense. Then I knew why they sounded so poor and things weren't going well at all. They wanted to let Moritz know, as he was the administrator of the estate that they were in dire need of that inheritance. I got to thinking then that George must have built up quite an estate, as when he died it sure rattled a lot of people on both sides of the Atlantic. Prior to this J. George Weber revelation, I had gone through a passel of old papers of my Grandpas that Katie had saved and there about 1918-1920 were receipts from a new Model "T" Ford touring car, a new corn binder, a new hay rake, a new hay loader, a new beet lifter, and a new cream separator and I thought at that time, how could they afford all this new stuff? Where did all this money come from? Now I knew! Good old George! The gold from California was a vineyard in the Napa Valley.

In with these letters from George was a report written by Moritz on the sequence of events dealing with George's death:

THE WEBER FAMILY OF BEAL CITY MICHIGAN

"In November 1915, I visited my brother George Weber, he was not married, near White Hall about 3 miles from St. Helena or 1 mile from Rutherford. In November 1916, some of the neighbors found him dead in bed. Eugene Webber (no relations) the coroner of Napa County telegraphed to me what to do. I wrote to him that George Weber left five heirs...this is myself, Moritz Weber, my sister's child Mrs. Mary Weber near Defiance, Ohio, my brother's children, Edward and Lizzie Weber near Defiance, Ohio, and my brother's 2 boys, Jacob and Joseph Weber in Germany, and my sister Walburga Seigel, also of Germany.

I and the two heirs in Ohio decided to sell the property. It was sold for about $5,600.00 to William Bradley, also of Germany. There was $1,300.00 cash in the bank at St. Helena, about $1,000.00 of this money was used to pay the expenses. In 1917, Jacob and Joseph Weber, my brother's boys and my sister Walburga Seigel of Germany sent a power of attorney to me that I should collect their money and send it to them. While this power of attorney was on the road, my sister died..

Mr. McClinic of Mt. Pleasant advised me to write to Germany to my sister's children Jacob Seigel and Mary Wieland that they should send a power of attorney to me. Mr. McClinic sent the two power of attorney's to Eugene L. Webber of Napa, California. The property was sold and I and the two heirs in Ohio each got $1,070.00. I got a letter from Germany a few days ago, they wrote that they did not get anything yet from the estate of George Weber. In Germany, my brother called him John George Weber *and here he called himself George Weber. I had to send some of my brother's letters to Eugene L. Webber of Napa and they all were signed George Weber. Sometime afterward the folks in Germany sent a power of attorney to a bank in San Francisco. They could not collect any money so they sent the power of attorney back to Germany."*

This narrative by Moritz creates another puzzle for me. Who is that heir, his sister's child Mrs. Mary Weber of Defiance, Ohio? I have no idea, if she is a Mrs., her name shouldn't be Weber. I doubt if I'll ever know, but there to be another sibling in that family and some of our branch of the clan did stay in Defiance, Ohio.

When Moritz went to visit George, he first went to San Diego and attended the International Panama-California Exposition. He wrote back that there were a lot of interesting things there but also a lot of bunk.

That $1,070.00 that Moritz and the heirs in Defiance got doesn't sound like much today, but in those days it could buy 3 automobiles and the bumpers to go on them as they were an accessory. Go buy 3 Fords today and you would spend $75,000.00. It was a nice piece of change.

I'm going to go back now and give some prior history on Germany so as to make it easier for you to understand the next segment of this inheritance business.

I mentioned before about the feelings of the German immigrants toward their "Old Country." They never wanted to look back to the miseries and oppression they suffered there. Germany was very militaristic and most German families raised their sons to be soldiers and they would follow their militaristic leaders anywhere to intimidate and gobble up their neighboring countries and they were always able to give the gullible world a sound reason for doing it. They did need this militaristic power in the past just for the defense of their homes and families, but they went too far the other way. The peaceful Germans then over the years immigrated to America. Many of them too went to Argentina, Brazil, and Canada, but most of them came here. I know my Grandfather Moritz was a peaceful man. Whenever there was trouble in the house, he headed out to cook beans.

Another point I want to bring out, there were no letters from Germany in the years prior to this inheritance business, if there had been any I'm sure they would have been saved along with the ones starting 1918 when the First World War ended.

We also must realize the conditions at that time. Travel was slow and no telephones. Those lawyers and officials in California well knew that Moritz the administrator would not go out there to supervise their actions, Moritz had to trust them. And since the American heirs had their money, the chance of the German heirs causing any trouble was very remote.

Here I am going to quote from just a few letters from Germany and it will help us see why I think Moritz was a little exasperated with those relatives and would just as soon get out of the whole deal. *"Walburga Seigel,*

Moritz's sister is suffering from water retention and knows she would not live long. She says she is getting very bad treatment from her son and his wife. He is very mean. He hit a horse so hard they had to slaughter it. He clubbed a calf and broke 2 legs and they had to slaughter that too. She locked herself in her room and her daughter-in-law broke down the door with an ax. She is praying the rosary now to be rotting in her grave before you get this letter. She is sorry she won't get any of the money as she will die, and he will get it all and he doesn't deserve it. There is much cursing and hard feelings as there is controversy over who is getting the money and the whole village is talking about it. Please don't tell them I write this letter to you they will make it rough on me."

In a letter from George Seigel, Walburga's husband saying his wife had died. He is now the heir as she died on 19 March 1919. He is in a hurry for the money as he is 71 years old and would like to have his peace and quiet.

"When I get the money I will share it with my 2 children Jacob and Marie. When you get the money should you send it right away or hold it awhile until one knows the situation better."

Now a letter from Marie Siegel, the daughter states: *"I beg to ask you why I and Brother Jacob were excluded from the inheritance from Uncle George. It would make us very happy to share in something from our mother's side. My father says "I will inherit the money" and we* can have some also. Please write if George had a will or not."

There is much more on this business in those letters. This next letter from Wallace Rutherford an attorney in Napa, California, explains how this inheritance business turned out.

.

WALLACE RUTHERFORD ATTORNEY-AT-LAW

MIGLIAVACCA BLDG.

NAPA, CAL.

February 6, 1924
   Mr. Moritz Weber
   Rosebush, Michigan

Dear Sir:

I received your letter sometime ago. When you sold your interest in the real property here in Napa, you did not leave your relations in Germany in very good shape. You sent a power of attorney to E.L. Webber at Napa and he in turn acted as attorney for the man to who you sold your interest. Instead of getting a deed direct from the heirs, Mr. Weber commenced an action in partition on behalf of the person to whom you sold and in that partition suit bid on the share of your relatives for a great deal less than he paid you. Mr. E.L. Webber collected the proceeds and instead of sending them to your relatives, retained them in his possession until your relatives sent a power of attorney to Mr. Lowey of San Francisco. Mr. Lowey then had to probate your sister's estate and collect money from Mr. Webber. After quite an effort that money was collected, but Mr. Webber has not yet paid to Mr. Lowey the money belonging to your nephews, but has promised to do so next week.

The balance of the money that was in the bank was paid to the alien Property Custodian and he still has it. Without doubt your relatives will get their money within the next two months.

WR; AH
Respectfully yours,

(Signature of Wallace Rutherford)

This letter was dated February 6, 1924, over eight years after George's death...Such Skullduggery!

Another point on the feeling of the emigrants to the old country: There was not one letter from Germany from the time they left in 1872 until this inheritance business came up in 1918, that was 46 years. I'm sure if a letter had been written it would have been saved along with the later ones. The letters then that started in 1918 gave Moritz reason to drag his feet and feel a bit of resentment to them. The First World War started in 1914 and ended in November of 1918. During this time there was little or no communication as we were at war with them.

During the First World War as in all wars, it is really amazing, the sacrifices the people willingly make to help the war effort. As the War dragged on and Germany started getting the bad end of it, everything was rationed and in short supply. Anything made of iron was collected and smelted down to make bullets and war materials. Toward the end, they even took all the bells out of the churches to make cannon balls.

It was really a shame as most churches had matched set of bells that rang beautifully together. It was a thing of pride to each village.

Following is a letter from Pastor Matt of Walhausen, Germany, the old family parish and he puts the touch on Moritz for money to get some bells in his belfry

Dear Mr. Weber,

I know from your sister-in-law, Anna that you have asked about me. She probably wrote you that I am 60 years old and am 23 years here. Like your sister-in-law, I too can write that she was very happy over what she received from you. And, what is the reason for my writing? Towards the end of the War we were forced to give away to the state our three church bells. It was a beautiful ringing set, newly installed in the year 1910. Through voluntary contributions we hope to buy soon three new bells. Now I like to do it, as so many other Priests have done it. I am asking for money from America. America has done so much for our poor Deutschland. Our bishop mentioned that too in his Lenten Message. I would be very happy and the whole parish too, if you would send a contribution to your home parish and buy the new bells.

Waldhausen, February 27, 1923
Reverently, Pastor Matt Deacon

Now on May 30, 1923 comes a letter of thanks to Moritz.

Dear Mr. Weber!
Today on May 29, I received your very much appreciated money. May God repay you is my wish and of the parish for you. On March 11, the bells were solemnly blest with the whole community participating and even people from the outside. We have now again beautiful ringing bells which are now paid for, thank God. The tower and roof has to be repaired, which will of course bring additional great expenses. Arlsberg had lost their larger bell also. They too installed a new bell at the same time that Waldhauser did.

For your brother George, shall holy masses be said, also for a happy death.

The situation in Deutschland is not good, our money is almost worthless. Should you see Frau Wagner there, please convey a "May God Bless You" from the heart. I worked with her brother, George Seigel for eight years, he was an accountant at a bank and was the manager. Again may God reward you for the money you gave.

THE WEBER FAMILY OF BEAL CITY MICHIGAN

Waldhauser May 30, 1923   *Reverently,*
                                Deacon Matt

Your sister-in-law Frau Anna Weber asks me to say greetings from her to you. She is not in good circumstances and is very thankful for all you do for her and give her.

This Frau Wagner he refers to is Barbara Wagner I wrote about in Chapter 3 and sister-in-law to Walburga Seigel.

In 1987, Charles Reihl, Raldon Pasch, and myself, went to Alaska with our motor home. We took 40 days and seen a lot of different country and many interesting things. On the return trip we came down through the Frazer Valley of British Columbia, then Washington, Oregon, and the Coastal highway down through California.

North of San Francisco, we drove inland and swung through the Napa valley. When we got to the point where George's property was, 3 miles South of St. Helena, we stopped and trod on the soil that he tilled. It was a very beautiful area and for me it was very emotional. There are Wineries all through the valley and most have wine-tasting rooms.

The Franciscan Winery, as near as I could figure was very near George's property. It is a beautiful place, we went in and dwelled a while sampling their wine. I bought a set of wineglasses on leaving.

There was a story in some magazine a bit ago on Napa Valley. It stated that a choice land there is selling for as high as one million dollars an acre.

The family should have hung on to the 26 acres of George's.

(Ed-. – Here Ben Weber's narrative ends, at a date unknown. Given the state of Mr. Weber's health, it is unlikely to be finished by him. - J.R.W.)

About the Author

A lifelong resident of Beal City, Michigan, Ben Weber was raised on the family farm in the northwest of the southeast quarter of Section 22, Town 15 North, Range 5 West, Nottawa Township, Isabella County Michigan, a quarter- mile north of the village. Ben was in the last class to graduate from the first St. Philomena High School in 1948.

In 1950, Ben's father John Jacob "Jake" Weber, bought a portable sawmill from a neighbor to provide activity and a livelihood for he and sons Ben, Jim, John and Ed, as the portable mill moved around the middle of Michigan sawing logs for hire by farmers. Jim Weber perished in an automobile accident in 1953.

In 1956, Ben and John Weber bought the mill from their father and established Weber Brothers Sawmill and Ed joined the partnership in 1966. In 1969, the partnership incorporated to become Weber Brothers Sawmill, Inc.. 1971 saw the sawmill burn down and a new mill was built at its present site.

Throughout his life Ben Weber has demonstrated a love of family and homeplace and worked to preserve the heritage of both. In 1975, the opening pages of the Beal City Area Centennial book contained the page at the right, dedicating the book to Ben Weber for his dedication of time and efforts to the Centennial. This book continues his legacy.

DEDICATION

Ben Weber

We, the Centennial Committee and writers of this History of Nottawa Township Area, are proud to dedicate this booklet to Ben Weber in recognition of his time and efforts generously given in behalf of the success of our Centennial.

www.ingramcontent.com/pod-product-compliance
Lightning Source LLC
Chambersburg PA
CBHW061334040426
42444CB00011B/2916